CW01044411

JACK JOHNSON VS. JAMES JEFFRIES

Robert Greenwood

JACK JOHNSON VS. JAMES JEFFRIES

THE PRIZE FIGHT
OF THE CENTURY

RENO, NEVADA, JULY 4, 1910

BY

ROBERT GREENWOOD

JACK BACON & COMPANY
RENO, NEVADA
2004

Library of Congress Control Number: 2004111312

ISBN 0-930083-13-X

Printed in the United States of America
by R.R. Donnelley & Sons

Designed by Jim Richards

Jack Bacon & Company
516 South Virginia Street
Reno, Nevada 89501

www.JackBacon.com

FIRST EDITION

Contents

PREFACE

In the language of boxing promotion, hyperbole has become commonplace, so much so that nearly every title fight is hailed as "The Fight of the Century." Seen in the light of history, however, it is the first title fight promoted under that banner that most deserves the honor. The contest between Jack Johnson and Jim Jeffries held in Reno, July 4, 1910 was, for several reasons, truly "The Fight of the Century." That fight attracted more public attention around the world than any since. For weeks prior to the event newspapers in every city in the land carried stories on almost every conceivable aspect of the fight. Magazines and newspapers sent their top correspondents to Reno to cover the contest, among them Jack London, John L. Sullivan, Bat Masterson, Rube Goldberg, Rex Beach and a host of others. Coverage was not limited to the United States. In England, France, Germany, Russia, Australia, Canada, South America, thousands of words were printed every day in the foreign press. On the day of the fight people across the nation watched facsimile re-enactments of the fight in auditoriums or on large electric billboards, or read bulletins posted outside newspaper offices. In exclusive clubs in New York City the rich and famous followed the fight by watching specially installed ticker-tapes. At matinee performances in theaters the latest bulletins were read to audiences between acts and during intermission.

It was Johnson's first title bout in the United States since he had won the heavyweight championship from Tommy Burns in Sydney, Australia in 1908. Many people underestimated Johnson's skills as a boxer and believed he had won the title through a fluke, a lucky punch, or a twist of fate. There was as a myth, common at the time, that black boxers had a "streak of yellow" in them, would not fight hard when pressed, and that Johnson was no exception. This, of course, was nonsense. He was the best defensive boxer the ring has known, his footwork was legendary, he was incredibly fast, and he had several punches he could deliver with telling power. Nat Fleischer, the distinguished boxing historian who had known and studied every champion from Jeffries to Marciano, and for many years editor of *Ring Magazine*, said he had no hesitation in naming Jack Johnson as the greatest of them all. By contrast, Jeffries was not so much a boxer as a heavy hitter, a man who could take much punishment and come back again and again. He had retired from the ring undefeated. In the months before the Reno fight he had trained hard to lose excess weight, hardening his body. Although he had been retired for five years, he had more ring experience than Johnson, and he was still a tough and dangerous opponent. Although sports writers at ringside wrote that it was not much of a fight, this is misleading because most of them favored Jeffries to win and were disappointed in his performance. The reason for their disappointment was because Jeffries could not land on Johnson. And the reason he could not was because of Johnson's defensive boxing skills. There was also grousing about too much clinching during the fight, done mostly by Jeffries, but they missed Johnson's skill at infighting, and the damage done to Jeffries in those exchanges. In a sense, the fight was a demonstration of brute force against skill, and skill won out. Jeffries was not at the peak of his powers, but he was the aggressor for most of the fight. Johnson was at the top of his form, never in better condition, and his strategy throughout the fight was intelligently planned. It was a contest between two great fighters, Jeffries on the one hand certainly one of the toughest and most dangerous champions in ring history, and Johnson, on the other, the greatest of all heavyweight boxers.

The fight broke all previous records for a sporting event. The gate was the largest ever recorded up to that time, with some 18,000 people in attendance, and not all who came could be seated. It was the largest purse for a prize fight - $100,000, with another $100,000 from motion picture rights. It brought about a renewed interest in boxing at a time when it was viewed with disfavor, banned in all states but Nevada, and when public interest in the sport had waned.

The focus of this book is upon the championship title fight in Reno, Nevada, July 4, 1910, the events leading up to it, and the events afterward. It was not my intention to write a biography of either Johnson or Jeffries, or to explicate the social *milieu* of America during those years. Events are presented as they occurred, in chronological order, and in an objective manner.

I wish to thank the following individuals and institutions who contributed so generously to this book. To Paul Elcano, of Reno, Nevada, who allowed me to make a large selection of photographs from his collection of Nevada post cards. To Gil Schmidtmann, of Mentone, California, who also gave permission to use several photographs from his collection. To Michael Holland, of Reno, Nevada, for use of his photograph of Jim Flynn. And to the Library of Congress, Washington, D.C., The Brooklyn Public Library, Brooklyn Collection, and the Chicago Historical Society for their permission to reproduce photographs from their collections.

To the Interlibrary Loan Department of the Clark County Library System, Las Vegas, Nevada, for supplying materials to my many requests. To Newton Baird, who read the manuscript in draft form, and offered valuable suggestions. To Rick Reviglio of Reno, Nevada for use of souvenir items and photographs from the fight and to the Nevada Historical Society of Reno, Nevada.

Robert Greenwood
Las Vegas, Nevada
June 8, 2004

Preliminaries

When James J. Jeffries won the world's heavyweight championship from Bob Fitzsimmons at Coney Island, New York, June 9, 1899, he proved himself to the boxing world a man of extraordinary strength and hitting power, the "iron man" of the ring. He was not a scientific boxer, but he was no mere slugger, either. Bob Fitzsimmons was no easy match; though he was thirty-six, he displayed dazzling footwork and a rapid punching style. He outboxed Jeffries for several rounds, but in the eleventh Jeffries delivered a series of hard punches that ended the round with a knockout. Jeffries was the new world's heavyweight champion, and would remain so for six years, until he retired from the ring in 1905, undefeated.

Jeffries knew nothing of Jack Johnson in 1899 – nor did anyone else – for that was the year Johnson had his first professional fight, in Chicago, a match he lost in six rounds. At that point in his career, Johnson had few if any boxing skills. He was a rough diamond, unpolished. His only asset was his speed – he was very fast, and one would suppose his first opponent, a black boxer whom

Johnson remembered only by the name of Klondike[1] threw a lot of punches before he landed the lucky one. The historic fight between Johnson and Jeffries in Reno, Nevada, was eleven years off in the future. For his part, Johnson would become determined as the years rolled by that one day their paths would cross. Jeffries, on the other hand, would prove reluctant.

Jeffries was born in Ohio in 1875 but grew up on a farm in southern California, where his father gave up farming and became an itinerant preacher. As a boy, Jeffries was famous for his rowdy behavior. Because of it he was expelled from school, and took up the trade of boilermaker. His first professional fight took place in San Francisco on July 2, 1896, when he knocked out Dan Long in two rounds.[2] The following year he wandered into James J. Corbett's training camp, where he was hired as a sparing partner for Corbett. By the time he was twenty-four he had worked his way to the position of top contender after only ten professional fights. In 1897-1898, he fought Henry Baker, Peter Everett, Bob Armstrong, and Tom Sharkey, the latter one of the toughest fighters of the time, beating them all. He had the ability to take the hardest blow on the point of his chin and still remain on his feet. His punches had terrific power behind them, carrying the mass of his great weight. He had developed a "crouch style," bent over with his head tucked between his shoulders, which made it difficult for his opponent to land a blow on his face, and in this manner he would advance relentlessly, driving straight blows to the body. He was slow, however, when compared to other boxers. In his fights with James J. Corbett and Bob Fitzsimmons, both of whom were noted for their excellent footwork, speed, and ring knowledge, Jeffries lasted out the early rounds in which they displayed superior boxing style. Both men could deliver rapid, staccato punches with force, but Jeffries simply bored in, rolling with the punches or absorbing them. When his opponents began to tire, Jeffries, drawing on his great recuperative powers, waited for the right moment to land his sledge-hammer blow. In these years he trained hard for his fights, and when he was not working out in some fashion, he was in the California mountains fishing for trout or hunting deer.

Meanwhile, Jack Johnson was struggling to make a name for himself. It was not an easy time for either boxers or the boxing profession. Prize fighting had fallen into disfavor with the general public, due largely to the efforts of social reformers who saw the sport as uncivilized and brutal. In most states it was illegal. In a few, exhibition matches were allowed, but with no prize money. In Pennsylvania, matches were limited to only a few rounds where no decision was permitted by the referee or judges. Such fights were called "no decision" contests, and the prize money, if any at all, was meager. This lack of money put the aspiring boxer at a disadvantage. He needed money to rent training facilities, hire sparring partners and trainers. In Pennsylvania the "no decision" law was rigidly enforced. In California, where the authorities were more tolerant, the law was not always enforced, and many fights were staged without interference.

Jack Johnson was born in Galveston, Texas, in March, 1878, had left school after completing the fifth grade to help support his parents, brothers and sisters, who were poor. At twelve, he left Galveston in a boxcar, dodging railroad police, to make his way in the world. In 1901, he returned to Galveston for a match with Joe Choyinski. It was not a triumphant return by any means. Johnson was still very much an unknown. Choyinski, however, had received some attention because he had fought boxers with recognized reputations. At the end of the third round police moved into the ring and stopped the fight. Both boxers were arrested and jailed for three weeks, neither one having enough money to post bail, as the prize money had been confiscated by police. Police had acted upon the Texas anti-boxing law. Soon after this episode, the Texas legislature passed another law making prize fighting a felony.[3] But the three weeks in jail were not a total loss for Johnson. The warden, as it turned out, liked boxing, as did the prisoners, and Choyinski and Johnson were allowed to put on exhibitions for their entertainment. Choyinski was a good teacher, and Johnson received some valuable instruction. A boxer with Johnson's deceptive speed, Choyinski knew, could become a superb defensive fighter. He told Johnson: "A man who can move like you should never have to take a punch. Don't try to block – you're fast enough to get clear out of the way."[4] Earlier, when Johnson had worked as a sparring partner for Joe Walcott, otherwise known as "the Barbados Demon" (not to be confused with the later Jersey Joe Walcott), he had begun to sharpen his defensive style. Walcott himself was known for his graceful style, and in teaching Johnson served as a kind of dance in-structor, as it were. Johnson himself would continue to polish his movements into a style uniquely his own.[5]

Johnson moved onto Colorado, where he met the great Tom Sharkey, a fighter with a national reputation. With him were Jack O'Brien, Spider Kelley, Tommy Ryan, and a few others who had managed to get a few fights at the Denver Coliseum. Sharkey hit upon the idea of organizing a boxing road show to give exhibitions for the price of a ticket. Sharkey selected the mining town of Cripple Creek for the opening performance. In the beginning the shows did well, but interest waned and the group found themselves in the hole financially. In an economy move, the boxers vacated the hotel and rented a miner's cabin on the outskirts of town. Johnson was appointed cook, a job that had its share of problems, particu-larly when their credit ran out and local merchants refused to fill Johnson's grocery basket. One by one the boxers gave it up, each going his own way, and the road show ended up where it had begun.[6]

Johnson then traveled to California, where a mild revival of interest in boxing was taking place. Police had relaxed their enforcement of ordinances and regulations, and contests were regularly scheduled in Los Angeles and San Francisco. In matches against George Gardner, Joe Kennedy, Hank Griffen, and others, Johnson earned some money, and for the first time in his boxing career his standard of living improved. His manager, Frank Corella, a boxing promoter from Bakersfield, signed him for a match in Los Angeles with Jack Jeffries (brother of James J. Jeffries, the reigning heavyweight champion), whom Johnson knocked out in five rounds. Sports writers began to take notice of Johnson, though some of them criticized what they considered to be his lackluster performances. He made boxing look too easy. 1902 was a big year for Johnson. He had a total of sixteen fights, of which four were draws, twelve were victories.

In those days a black boxer had another problem to contend with. It was called the color line. It was similar to baseball, where black players played in a separate league, white players in another. For boxers it usually meant that black fighters fought each other. However, this was not always the case. Among lower-ranked contenders, a black boxer would occasionally fight a white, as was the case when Johnson fought Jack Jefferies. But blacks were excluded from the big purses, the championship fights in the heavyweight division. Former champion John L. Sullivan had said he would never fight a black boxer, and he never did. Some of the best boxers of the time were blacks: Sam McVey, Denver Ed Martin, Frank Childs, Black Bill, Joe Jeanette, Sam Langford, and others. Many people – including the social reformers of the time – feared that a title fight between a black and a white boxer might carry racial overtones, suggesting racial supremacy for the victor, with the potential for igniting racial conflict. Reformers also deplored what they called the brutal spectacle of boxing, equally denouncing the purse money as crass commercialism, overlooking the fact that it was one of the few activities in which blacks could earn large sums of money. Rednecks said that blacks should be "kept in their place" and not mix with whites. These notions provided grounds for resentment among black people, and white people too, who saw boxing as a test of skill and strength between two individuals, and not as symbols of race. But these people were in the minority. Johnson made this point in an interview with a reporter shortly before the Johnson-Jeffries fight:

> *It was not my fights themselves, but my fight to get those fights that proved the hardest part of the struggle. It was my color. They told me to get a "rep"; but how was I to get a "rep" without meeting fighters of class? But I made them fight me. I just kept plugging along, snapping up what chances to fight I could grab, until by and by the topnotchers saw that, sooner or later, they'd have to take me on. As soon as I had shown what I could do, the fight public – most of the fans anyway – took sides with me, and that helped a whole lot.*[7]

Johnson described the years 1903-1904 as "dull" – perhaps because of a lighter schedule. He had seven matches in 1903, only four in 1904. Of these, he said only four were significant: a six-round "no decision" match with Black Bill in Philadelphia, a twenty-round contest with Sam McVey in San Francisco, a six round match with Frank Childs in Chicago, and a knockout over Denver Ed Martin in Los Angeles.[8] All these opponents were excellent black boxers. Sports writers could see there was something unusual in Johnson's style. He boxed so gracefully it seemed at times he was dancing, not boxing. His reflexes were so quick that his movements seemed sometimes blurred. He was gaining his "rep" – but not everyone applauded his style. If he dodged punches, feinted beautifully and then countered with a lightening hook, dancing away from his opponent, there were those who said he was "showing off." Sometimes he was the object of boos, whistles, and catcalls by those who could not or would not appreciate his technique, who wanted to see him driven into the ropes, or flat on the canvas. Some sports writers felt that he never extended himself to his limits, reached deep for extra reserves – but then he rarely had to. As he grew more confident he sometimes engaged in a repartee with his opponents or with fans sitting ringside, flashing his gold-toothed smile. This annoyed those who saw it as buffoonery, not taking the sport seriously enough, and in the case of an unfortunate opponent, adding insult to injury. To such observers this verbal taunting was a barb tinged with racial overtones and downright arrogance. Others said it might be excused on the grounds that Jack Johnson, like most of his race, was basically fun-loving and simple-minded. It was, of course, nothing more that Johnson's sense of humor and wit, with a bit of clowning.

On March 28, 1905, Johnson met Marvin Hart, a white heavyweight with a lackluster record. The fight was held in San Francisco. Early in the match Johnson unleashed an uppercut that knocked Hart out of the ring. Hart managed to climb back in and the referee signaled the fight to continue. Johnson was never in any trouble during the twenty rounds the fight lasted. To some observers he even appeared to be carrying Hart into the final rounds so as to give the fans full value for their money. Hart hardly laid a glove on Johnson. But when the referee announced his decision – much to Johnson's astonishment – he held up Hart's arm as the winner. Many of the fans applauded the decision either because they had bet on Hart, or because they wanted to see Johnson get his come-uppance. About the only fans to protest were those who had bet on Johnson, and they were in minority. Johnson said later it had all been a mistake, that in the excitement of the moment the referee raised the wrong arm and when he realized his mistake, refused to correct it.[9] Others have suggested the referee had accepted money from the gamblers to announce Hart the winner.[10] Whatever the reason, it would delay Johnson's shot at the championship by two years. To explain why this is so, we must return to Jim Jeffries and his decision to retire as the reigning heavyweight champion in 1905.

After Jeffries had won the title from Bob Fitzsimmons in 1899, he defended his title only ten times. He fought Jack Finnegan in 1900 and 1903, Hank Griffen in 1902, Joe Kennedy and Gus Ruhlin in 1901, Bob Fitzsimmons for a re-match in 1902, and Jack Munroe twice, in 1903 and 1904. The most important match was with Tom Sharkey, at Coney Island, November 3, 1899, which lasted twenty-five rounds. Sharkey was perhaps the gamest fighter of his time; no matter how much punishment he had taken, he would simply not go down. The fight was held under intense lights so as to make moving pictures, hung so low over the ring that Jeffries said he could reach up and touch them with his glove. Jeffries said: "I did not think it possible for lights to make so much heat. It was like standing at the mouth of a blast furnace and hotter than the blast from a locomotive when the fire door is opened."[11] It was a savage fight: both men were injured and exhausted. Jeffries had suffered a broken arm. Sharkey had three broken ribs and severe cuts over one eye and ear. He was taken to a hospital after the fight and Jeffries was told by New York police not to leave the city until Sharkey was out of danger.[12] Shortly after this fight, and because reformers were enraged over so much blood and sweat spilled on the canvas, prize fighting was declared illegal in New York.

Jeffries felt that he had taken on all comers and beat them all, ignoring, of course, the black heavyweights, notably Jack Johnson. But Jeffries had not been consistent in drawing the color line. In 1898, before he won the title from Bob Fitzsimmons, he had fought black heavyweight Peter Jackson in San Francisco, and won in only three rounds. As 1904 drew to a close, Jeffries was convinced there were no more heavyweights left for him to meet:

Besides that the fight game was in bad condition in 1905. Practically every state in the United States had put a ban on boxing. New York, Chicago, Pittsburgh, St. Louis, Cincinnati and other of the large cities forbade the sport. The only state that tolerated even twenty round contests was California and, out there, I was considered unbeatable and no one would consider matching against me... There were no heavyweights anywhere on the horizon.[13]

There was Jack Johnson, of course, but as Marvin Hart had been given the decision over Johnson by the referee, Jeffries felt Johnson did not merit a shot at the title. Jeffries announced his intention to retire from the ring. In those days it was customary for champions to cash in on their fame by touring the vaudeville circuit, and Jeffries was no exception. He signed a lucrative contract to appear as Davy Crockett in a road show, turned in his boxing gloves for a raccoon cap, and went on tour. When he returned to California, he bought an alfalfa farm near Burbank, and settled down to the life of a gentleman farmer. He also speculated in real estate, turning a profit, and opened a saloon and restaurant in Los Angeles bearing his name.

What Jeffries had done was unprecedented. No heavyweight champion before him had vacated the title by retiring. Sports writers put on their thinking caps and began speculating on how a new champion could be crowned. It seemed a dilemma. In those days there were no official rankings and no boxing commissions to arrange the transition, so it was left to managers and promoters. What transpired was a series of somewhat confusing events that did nothing to resolve the matter. Two boxers, Marvin Hart and Jack Root, were promoted by their managers in such a way as to put them in the limelight as contenders for the vacant title. Jeffries was persuaded to referee the bout. Some sources have said that Jeffries either arranged or sanctioned the match, that he chose both Hart and Root, either one of whom was acceptable to him as the new champion. The national press, probably at the urging of managers and promoters, began to herald the fight as for the heavyweight championship title, and that Jeffries, as official referee, would pass the title by raising the winner's hand.

Jeffries told a different version. He referred to the match as a "mythical championship," and that he had agreed to act as referee as a favor to an old friend, Lou Houseman, Root's manager. Contradicting himself, Jeffries said he had no right to confer the title in such a manner, yet agreed to do it as a favor for a friend. Confusing the matter further, he said: "The only way anyone should be declared a champion is by fighting and beating the champion."[14]

Despite the publicity, only 5,000 spectators showed up for the fight in Reno. Nevada was then the only state in which prize fighting had not been declared illegal. The purse was a paltry $5,000, and proof – if any were needed – that prize fighting had fallen upon hard times. Of the two men, Root was the better boxer and easily won the first eleven rounds. But he tired in the twelfth and Hart landed a lucky punch, knocking him out. Jeffries had lifted Hart's hand, and the title, although a clouded one, passed to Hart. But it was a title nevertheless, and Jeffries had sanctioned it by his presence and officiating as a referee. As the new champion, Hart brought nothing to boxing. He had no charisma, no style, no panache.

Johnson must have been frustrated by this turn of events. Though Jeffries and others had passed over him as a contender for the title (because of Hart's earlier decision over Johnson), those who understood the temper of the times knew that Johnson had been excluded because he was black. Had Johnson been a white boxer he probably would have had his shot at the title. Meanwhile, he busied himself with a series of fights in Philadelphia, where matches were limited to six rounds, and where the fees were small, meeting Black Bill, Joe Jeanette, Morris Harris, Jim Jeffords, all black boxers. If this was to be his fate, its limits described by an autocratic society, he wanted no part of it. His mind was set on becoming champion. To that end he would travel the earth, issuing challenges, and outraging social convention.

Marvin Hart held the title for only one year. There then appeared on the scene a French-Canadian by birth, Noah Brusso, who chose to call himself Tommy Burns, the name he is remembered by in boxing history. He was born in Canada in 1881 and later moved to Detroit, where he won local fame as an accomplished lacrosse player. He first attracted attention as a boxer when he knocked out Philadelphia Jack O'Brien in Los Angeles in 1903. In 1906 he met Marvin Hart and won. Burns, the new champion, was a game fighter with a contentious boxing style. He was a bit over five feet seven in height and weighed at his heaviest only 175 pounds – light for a heavyweight – but he was a hard hitter, broad in the chest and shoulders. In 1907, he traveled to England and beat some of the best, including Gunner Moir, former British champion. He defended his title successfully several times in 1907 and 1908. He astonished the boxing world when he knocked out Jem Roche, the Irish champion, in just eighty-eight seconds, setting a new record for the shortest heavyweight fight ever. Sports writers, growing more respectful of Burns, took a second look at the new champion.

Johnson was interested in extending his reputation beyond the United States, and so in 1907 he sailed for Australia. At the time there was a dispute over the Australian heavyweight championship by two contenders for the title, Peter Felix, a black boxer, and Bill Lang. Johnson settled the dispute, in a manner of speaking, by knocking both men out, Felix in one round, and Lang in nine rounds.[15] The Australians took a liking to Johnson, his colorful personality and flamboyant persona, and he was warmly welcomed and given many receptions. One story that Johnson told of his stay in Australia reveals his sense of humor, and the Aussies must have loved it.

He had gone to the races at the track in Melbourne, accompanied by Jim Brennan, who had promoted Johnson's fight against Peter Felix. He decided to bet five dollars, all the pocket money he said he had on him, on Brennan's horse, a filly called Istria. Johnson placed his bet with one of the track bookies, was recognized by several people in the crowd who waved greetings to him, and he waved back. This exchange of greetings went on until the horses were in the starting gate. Istria won the race, and Johnson went up to the bookie and collected his winnings. To his amazement, the bookie handed him a large roll of bills, far in excess of what a five dollar ticket would bring. Then other bookies came up to him, handing him large rolls of bills. One of them said to him: "I say, Mr. Johnson, you were lucky to bet so much on that horse." Johnson says he then realized that his waving to his friends was taken by the bookies as bets placed, a custom still in practice today, where signals are transmitted by waving arms and hands, in semaphore fashion. Johnson said he had to buy a handbag to carry the money, there was so much of it. When he arrived at his hotel room, he counted the money and discovered that by waving and greeting his friends at the track, he had, unexpectedly, become $15,000 richer.[16]

At best, this story must be taken as a tall-tale, the kind Johnson loved to amuse listeners with, or as an exaggeration of a small truth. His autobiography contains many such stories, and readers must not rely upon them as the literal truth. Another Australian adventure describes a footrace with a wild kangaroo. Someone had bet Johnson that he could not outrun a kangaroo. He covered the bet. Johnson and the kangaroo took their places at the starting line, and they were off over a flat plain, running at top speed. The race went on for some distance, until the kangaroo, spent and exhausted, collapsed on the ground. Johnson collected his bet.

Although Johnson had hoped for a championship match with Tommy Burns after his Australian tour, another two years would pass before that event occurred. In 1908, Johnson followed Burns to England and issued another challenge. But Burns managed to dodge Johnson, making excuses. He said that Johnson did not merit a shot at the title because Hart had won a referee's decision over Johnson, and that he, Burns, had won the championship from Hart. He said the purse was below his usual earnings. He said the proposed contract was not satisfactory – or whatever. Burns was given to loud talk and bluster. He shouted his own praises with such conviction that many people believed him. He played the part of world champion in a somewhat royal manner, always trailing a retinue of admirers when he entered a saloon or theater, holding impromptu court for sports writers, and mouthing opinions as proclamations.

At one point while both men were in England it seemed a match might be in the offing. The National Sporting Club, which sponsored all the important matches in England, had indicated it might be interested, and agreed to a meeting with Sam Fitzpatrick, Johnson's manager. Fitzpatrick had thought the prestige of such a distinguished sporting association might be able to persuade Burns to enter the ring against Johnson. He had also thought there was no color line in England. But that notion was demolished when Johnson was refused entrance to the club and kept waiting outside while Fitzpatrick carried on negotiations. In any case, the club offered a purse of only five hundred pounds, with both fighters expected to pay their own expenses, an offer that was unacceptable to both Johnson and Burns. About this time the Prince of Wales, the contemporary arbiter of sporting matters in England, made the remark that Burns should give Johnson fairer treatment, and that

Burns was a "Yankee Bluffer." (Actually he was a Canadian.) The press took notice of anything the royal Prince said, and the remark was widely quoted.

Always aware of his role as white heavyweight champion of the world, Burns now began to make disparaging remarks about Johnson, saying he had a "yellow streak." He had also drawn the color line, and he was hostile toward Johnson because he was black.[17] Perhaps this was just another subterfuge Burns used to avoid a match with Johnson, perhaps not. Such hostility was not limited to white champions before and after Burns. In those days openly prejudiced remarks were commonplace: epithets and racial slurs regularly appeared in newspapers, cartoons, and books. One contemporary boxing historian wrote of Johnson: "He was by no means unintelligent, and, not without good reason, was regarded generally with the greatest possible dislike. With money in his pockets and physical triumph over white men in his heart, he displayed all the gross and overbearing insolence which makes what we call the buck nigger insufferable."[18]

Certainly Johnson was intelligent; intelligent enough to know how prejudice worked against blacks in the boxing game, and, as it turned out, intelligent enough to win in spite of it:

> *While sporting writers and boxing authorities still continued to question my claim to higher ring honors, it certainly was not because my record as a boxer was in any wise questionable. I had demonstrated my strength, speed and skill, but still faced many obstacles, the principal one of which was the customary prejudice because of my race. Had it not been for these prejudices, which I shall not discuss here, I think I would have been instrumental in making an entirely different history of boxing in the United States and the world, from that which has been recorded. With the beginning of 1907 I had attained a success that I believed entitled*

me to propose myself as an aspirant for the championship. Tommy Burns held the coveted honor and I began to direct my attention toward him. It was two years before I got to him and proved my abilities by winning the championship.[19]

Meanwhile, some sports writers began to wonder whether Burns might be procrastinating. Perhaps the Prince of Wales was right. Maybe Burns was a bluffer. In any case, there would be no match in England.

The Fight
at Rushcutter's Bay

If a match between Burns and Johnson were to occur, it would require a promoter of unusual abilities: a man of wealth, a flair for the spectacular and with unflappable composure. Such a man was Hugh D. McIntosh, an Australian with the reputation for making extraordinary deals. Indeed, his nickname was "Huge Deal" McIntosh. He was a former bicycle racer, Member of Parliament, owned a large portion of the lucrative British milk bar business, and had lately become interested in promoting prize fights. He arranged a meeting with Sam Fitzpatrick and Tommy Burns' representative, Billy Neal, and presented plans for a match at Rushcutter's Bay, on the outskirts of Sydney. He promised to build a huge stadium for the event that would attract boxing fans all over Australia, and the fight would be held on the day after Christmas, 1908. Burns demanded a guarantee of $30,000, win or lose, and he would not fight for less. McIntosh agreed, and the color line fell. Johnson, however, was guaranteed only $5,000, win or lose, a sum that was surely an affront to his pride. But it was the match he had waited years for, an opportunity he might never have again, so he shook off his aggravation, smiled his golden smile, and signed the contract. Johnson and Fitzpatrick, short of funds, found an inexpensive training camp at the Sir Joseph Banks Hotel in Botany Bay, not as opulent as the Hydro Majestic Hotel at Medlow Bath, where Burns had set up, but adequate for their needs. Johnson trained hard. He ran long distances every morning, boxed with his sparring partner, Bill Lang, practiced with the medicine ball, punched the bags, and did the cakewalk for sports writers.

The public had made Burns the favorite in the betting by a 5-4 margin. Burns was his usual loud self, talking about Johnson's "yellow streak," and his inability to take a hard punch. When told about the odds against him, Johnson, confident of victory, said to his manager, Sam Fitzpatrick: "It's the best chance I'll ever have of cleaning up. And I haven't a pound. We owe the hotel bill still."[1]

Though a contract had been signed, Johnson continued to have differences with Burns and McIntosh. There was the matter of who would referee the fight. There had been rumors the fight was fixed in favor of Burns, and some of these had been printed in the Australian and American press. There was also the possibility that Australian police might stop the fight, resulting in a "no contest" decision. Johnson wanted to make certain the fight was fair, and that the referee, not the police, would make the decision on who was the winner. In a meeting with Burns and McIntosh, which grew heated when no agreement was reached, Burns insulted and cursed Johnson, and moved as if to strike him with a chair. McIntosh intervened, took the chair from Burns, also a heavy inkwell which Burns had snatched from a desk and aimed at Johnson. Johnson then played his hole card. He asked the angry Burns if McIntosh would be acceptable as the referee. Taken by surprise, Burns looked at McIntosh and said, yes, of course. McIntosh, equally surprised, said he had little experience as a referee but would take the job if both men insisted.[2] Johnson's judgment was that McIntosh would be fair and honest, and in this he was correct. McIntosh even read the Queensbury book of rules on boxing before the fight to qualify himself. When the news came out that McIntosh was to referee, the first reaction of the public was one of disbelief. They could not believe that an arrangement so friendly to Burns was true. The betting odds immediately changed from 5-4 in favor of Burns to 7-4, making him the clear favorite.

During his earlier tour of Australia in 1907, Johnson had won respect from some boxing fans and become an object of amusement for others. But this fight at Rushcutter's Bay for the world's championship was another matter, matching a white champion against a black challenger. The prejudice against Johnson in Australia never reached the intensity that it did in the Unites States, but it was there nonetheless. An editorial writer in *Sydney's Illustrated Sporting* and *Dramatic News* wrote: "Citizens who have never prayed before are supplicating Providence to give the white man a strong right arm with which to belt the coon into oblivion."[3] Protestant reformers denounced the fight from the pulpit and charged it would surely corrupt the morals of Australian youth. Racist posters appeared on walls around Sydney depicting a game but undersized white man squaring off against an enormous black man, with a printed message that read: "this battle may in the future be looked back upon as the first great battle of an inevitable race war..."[4]

The event at Rushcutter"s Bay was a first in several respects. It was the first time a fight for the world's heavyweight championship had been held outside the United States. It was the first time the promoter of a fight had acted as referee. And, most significantly, it was the first time a black boxer had fought a white champion for the title. On the morning of the fight some twenty thousand people converged on the huge wooden structure that McIntosh had built. Outside the stadium was a gauntlet of food vendors, hawkers, hustlers, and gate crashers. The most famous of all gate crashers, "One-eyed Connolly," sat near ringside, having pulled off a scam to get his seat. There was a small army of sports writers, many representing newspapers from around the globe, including John L. Sullivan, who covered the fight for the *New York Times.* Jack London, the celebrated novelist, represented the *New York Herald.* London and his wife had been touring the South Pacific on their yacht, the *Snark,* and had arrived at Sydney in time for the fight. The stadium was filled to capacity, with thousands standing outside. A contingent of police stood at ringside, ready to stop the fight should an unmerciful mauling of one of the contestants occur. But Burns, Johnson, and McIntosh had all agreed beforehand that the "no contest" decision would not be given. It would be the referee's prerogative to declare the winner based on points or a knockout. Burns was confident he would win. Johnson was supremely confident but chaffed by the sacrifices he had made to get to the fight: the small share of the purse, the long history of insults aimed at him by Burns, the years of delay and haggling in arranging for the match. Johnson felt that Burns had something coming to him, and his strategy was to extend the fight and punish Burns as much as possible to give him full value for his $30,000 (Burns' share of the purse).[5] Another reason was because of the film rights: fans did not want to pay to see a film of a fight that lasted only a few rounds. They expected more.

Johnson was the first to enter the ring. There were some cheers from those who remembered his fights against Peter Felix and Bill Lang in Sydney and Melbourne in 1907, but there were also catcalls and jeers. Johnson unfurled his robe with a grand gesture, much in the manner of a bullfighter (he would later in life become one), bowed to the audience and smiled his golden smile. He appeared completely at ease, indifferent to those who jeered. A loud roar went up as Burns climbed through the ropes. Oddly, he was dressed in a street suit. He briefly acknowledged the cheering, removed the suit, hitched up his dark boxing trunks, and talked to his corner men. McIntosh motioned the two men toward the center of the ring and cautioned them against what would not be allowed. Johnson noticed a bandage on Burns' right arm. "Tell him to take that off," Johnson said to McIntosh. McIntosh was exasperated that another point of contention had come up at the last minute. "You come out fighting when the bell rings," McIntosh replied, "or I will disqualify you." But Johnson was adamant. "I want that bandage off or I put my robe back on. There will be no fight." Burns looked non-plussed, removed the bandage, and the crowd roared for the fight to begin.[6] Then the two boxers touched gloves and walked back to their corners, waiting for the bell.

Burns threw a few long punches, but Johnson easily danced away. Johnson had the longer reach and hit Burns with several straight lefts. He then feinted a long left, lowered his right shoulder, pivoted, and brought up a right uppercut that knocked Burns to the canvas. A hush fell over the stadium. The unexpected had happened. Was it simply a lucky punch? Burns lay still as the count began, then rolled over and rose to his feet at the count of eight. The crowed cheered. Burns, shaken by the uppercut, went into a crouch and hammered at Johnson's midsection. Johnson pushed him away and delivered a right cross to Burns' chin, staggering him. Before the first round ended Burns managed to hit Johnson with a weak punch on the jaw, but to no effect. When the bell rang ending the first round, few supposed Burns had much chance of winning. But Burns was cocky and game, determined to do his best.

As the second round began, Johnson connected with a left to Burns' chin. Burns appeared to stumble and his ankle turned so that he fell but quickly recovered, only to receive another left to his eye, which began to swell. Johnson finished the round with a hard right to Burns' stomach. It was easily Johnson's round, and he danced back to his corner, grinning widely at spectators ringside.

The third round opened at close quarters, Burns driving short punches to Johnson's ribs, Johnson driving hard punches to Burns' midsection. Johnson danced away and continued to hit Burns with jabs, all the while putting on a masterful display of defensive boxing. In the fourth round Johnson called out to Burns: "Find that yellow streak. You have had much to say about it; now uncover it."[7] Burns mumbled insults in reply and went into his crouch. Taunting him, Johnson dropped his arms to his side, extended his chin as a target and invited Burns to hit him, if he could. Burns, angered, swung wildly, off balance, missed, and covered as Johnson let go with another straight left to the eye. In the seventh round Johnson began to hurt Burns, calling out to the audience: I thought Tommy was an in-fighter. Come on, Tommy, swing your right." "Yellow dog," Burns shouted back.[8] Toward the end of the round Johnson floored Burns with a terrific right to the body. The fight was now Johnson's and he knew it. Burns' eyes were swollen, he was bleeding from the mouth, he was tiring, and Johnson was all over him.

As Johnson toyed with Burns, he glanced into the crowd, watching the expressions on faces, sometimes exchanging remarks, when he noticed at the very back of the stadium a black man sitting on a fence watching every movement of the fight. This man caught Johnson's attention.

He was one of a very few black men present. Every time Johnson made a move, the black man mimicked it, swinging a left or a right, ducking, as though in the ring himself. But his pantomime of the fight came to an abrupt end when Johnson ducked unusually low to avoid a haymaker by Burns, and, attempting to follow the movement, fell off the fence. Johnson was so amused he laughed and flashed his golden smile. Jack London and his wife, Charmian, were at ringside, and London took special notice of that smile. According to Johnson, it was on that occasion that London got the idea of the "golden smile," a phrase he used frequently in his descriptions of Johnson.[9] A bit of trivia may be appropriate here. Of the twenty thousand people who watched the fight, only two women were present (who were not identified at the time), and writers in recent years have wondered about the identity of these two women. Johnson has solved part of the mystery, identifying Mrs. London as one.

Johnson knew Burns would never quit so long as he could stand, so in the following rounds he hit him with lefts and rights, but never hard enough to knock him out. He was giving Burns his $30,000 worth. By the tenth round Burns' eyes had swollen to the point he could barely see. His movements had slowed, his punches were weak, and he continued to bleed from his mouth. In the thirteenth round the police at ringside were growing restless, seeing that Burns had, for all practical purposes, lost the fight, and thinking perhaps Burns might suffer serious injury were the fight to continue. But Burns had noticed, and cried out for them not to interfere, that he was not hurt. When the bell rang for the fourteenth round, Burns aimed a straight right at Johnson and missed. Johnson responded with a hard right to the jaw and Burns fell to the canvas. He rose with difficulty at the count of eight, his guard low, obviously exhausted. The police stopped the fight and McIntosh pointed to Johnson, the new champion.

After the fight, Burns complained to anyone who would listen that had not the police intervened, he would have defeated Johnson. But this was the garrulous Tommy Burns, trying to mitigate with words what he could not accomplish in the ring. It was reported in Australian newspapers in the week following the fight that Burns lost his share of the purse at the race track in Sydney. But that is unlikely. Two years later another report stated Burns had saved as much as $100,000 from his career in the ring, which would have made him a wealthy man, given the value of the dollar in those days. In 1908 and 1909, he had several fights in England and

France. And in 1910, he turned up in Reno for the Johnson-Jeffries fight, where he loudly declared that Jeffries would give Johnson the beating of his life.

There was hardly a scratch on Johnson. After he returned to his camp at Botany Bay he took a swim in the surf, a motor drive along the coast, and in the evening entertained friends at dinner. Meanwhile, Jack London had cabled his report of the fight to the *New York Herald* in which he said there was no fight, that it was a contest between a pigmy and a colossus, a funeral for Burns, where Johnson acted as undertaker, grave-digger and sexton, all in one. He said Burns never landed a blow (not quite accurate), that his situation was hopeless and preposterous. In closing, London wrote: "But one thing now remains. Jim Jeffries must now emerge from his alfalfa farm and remove that golden smile from Jack Johnson's face. Jeff, it's up to you. The White Man must be rescued." [10]

Reveling in his victory, Johnson stayed on for a while in Australia. He was offered a contract for a vaudeville tour, and he accepted, earning more from his stage appearances than he had from his fight with Burns. He partied with his Australian friends, bet the horses at the race track, and began to play the role of world's heavyweight champion as he thought it should be played, which was at loggerheads with what the public expected, especially of a black champion. In creating this new image of himself, one of his first acts was to fire his manager, Sam Fitzpatrick. This created something of a stir in the boxing world. Fitzpatrick's was a respected name; he had played a key roll in arranging the match with Burns, and he and helped to finance Johnson's pursuit of Burns around the world. The break was seen by many sports writers as the act of an ungrateful and arrogant Johnson who had used his manager to gain his own ends, and having achieved those ends discarded him as one might discard a soiled handkerchief. For his part, Johnson may have felt he wanted more control over arranging matches and handling the money. Fitzpatrick, on the other hand, had become disturbed by the outward change in Johnson's personality, a change he knew would outrage the general public, especially the social reformers. He told reporters in Vancouver that the Jack Johnson who would step off the boat would not be the same Jack Johnson they had known earlier. Johnson had begun to appear in public with Hattie McLay, a New York Irish girl,[11] whom he had introduced as "my wife." They were not married, but it was Johnson's idiosyncrasy to call whatever woman he was going with at the time as "my wife." He did this routinely up to the time he married Etta Duryea in 1911. In any case, Fitzpatrick and Hattie McLay did not get on well, and it may have been her influence that caused the break between Johnson and Fitzpatrick.

Johnson then took his revenge against the National Sporting Club in England by canceling his contract to fight Sam Langford in London, in February, 1909.[12] No doubt Johnson remembered the indignity of having to wait outside the club on the sidewalk while Sam Fitzpatrick had negotiated for him. But all Johnson said was that the contract was invalid because it had been negotiated by Fitzpatrick, who no longer represented him. The British considered this intolerable, an affront to the dignity of a grand old institution, one they would not forget. But Johnson cared nothing for the dignity of grand old institutions. He gave as good as he got. He had elevated that maxim to an art inside the ring. Why not extend it outside the ring, to the world at large?

CONTRADICTIONS

Those who believed the public image of a champion should be one of humility were not pleased with Jack Johnson. Johnson was not a man to bow and scrape before others. He had been born poor. His father was a janitor in a Galveston, Texas school, and he had three sisters and a brother. He had often helped his father with his janitorial work after school, as his father suffered a slight paralysis in his legs. He had run away from home at the age of twelve to make his way in the world, and had survived by his wits. When he could not afford something he needed – even a coat to keep warm – he did without. His early lifestyle was unremarkable, as undistinguished as the life of transients described by Jack London in his book, *The Road*. But now he had money and fame. He could afford champagne, motor cars, expensive cigars, diamond rings and furs for his ladies. To his critics this outward display of wealth was irksome enough, but coupled with his indifference for social conventions, it was outrageous. He liked to drive fast, ignored speed laws, and was arrested many times, cheerfully paying his fine in a court from a roll of hundred dollar bills. Stories began to make the rounds, telling of wild parties long into the night, drunken revelries and sexual adventures, no doubt embellished with each new telling.

Confident of himself, Johnson was very much an individual who spoke his own mind, and this was interpreted by his critics as arrogance and insolence. When his photograph appeared in the newspapers, dressed in a tailored suit cut in the latest fashion, sporting a gold-knobbed cane, flashing his golden smile, they said, "Jack Johnson is a dandy" – or worse. Some, who were patronizing or of a malicious bent, attributed this to a simple-minded and childlike nature, which they described as characteristic of his race. When he began to appear in public with Hattie McLay, a white woman, many were outraged, and saw him, in the idiom of the day, as a "Bad Nigger." Hattie herself was not exactly a model of decorum. She was drunk much of the time. She drank so much that Johnson complained she was an embarrassment to him.[1] She had traveled with Johnson to Australia for his fight with Tommy Burns, returned with him to Vancouver, and on to Chicago. It was there they parted company when Johnson discovered a cache of liquor she had hidden under the mattress of her bed. He may have thought he was rid of her, but the women in his life had a way of turning up at the most inopportune moment.

Earlier, when he had been fighting his way up through the ranks, he had become infatuated with Clara Kerr, a black girl whom he had met in Philadelphia. She traveled with him to Chicago and California. An old acquaintance of Johnson's, William Bryant, a horse trainer, had come to the coast, and Johnson introduced him to Clara. Clara took a fancy to Bryant. While Johnson was in training, Bryant escorted Clara to the race track and introduced her to his sporting crowd. Unknown to Johnson, they were having an affair. One night when he returned to his hotel room after a fight, he found they had left, taking with them everything he owned. "I was dumbfounded," Johnson said. "A woman whom I greatly loved had fled from me, but this time the cause, instead of a trifling domestic dispute, was another man. The shock unnerved me. For this first time in my life my faith in friends and humanity had been shaken to the foundation."[2] Determined to get her back, he learned they had gone to Arizona, and finding them there, he persuaded Clara to return with him to Chicago. But their reconciliation was brief. Again Clara disappeared, taking with her what money and valuables Johnson had left in the hotel room. Many years later, when Johnson had become famous, he learned that Clara had been arrested for murder and was being held in prison in Tom's River, New Jersey, waiting trial. Though he no longer had any romantic feeling for her (he was involved with other women at that time of his life), he did go to see her, and hired an attorney to defend her. He had no legal obligation to Clara, as they had never married, and considering that she had twice robbed him, little moral obligation. When she was acquitted and out on the streets with no means of support, Johnson bought for her a small boarding hotel which she operated successfully for many years.[3] In coming to her aid, Johnson displayed the good side of his nature, which could be generous to a fault.

When Johnson parted with Hattie McLay, he was introduced to the flesh pots of Chicago's Levee District by George Little. Little had previously worked in the Levee for a political boss, seemingly knew everyone there, and was only too happy to act as Johnson's personal tour guide. Johnson was then without a manager, Little knew it, and by catering to Johnson's whims saw his opportunity to become not only his manager but a national sporting figure as well. He would realize both ambitions. Little had access to every establishment in the Levee, including the Everleigh Club, the most elegant whorehouse in America, run by two southern ladies with an aristocratic background.[4] The place was furnished in opulent splendor, with it's own bar, restaurant, and ballroom, where the rich and

famous could pick and choose from among some of the most beautiful prostitutes to be found anywhere. Minna and Ada Everleigh
were themselves the very souls of discretion, so that politicians,
judges, bankers, could patronize the whorehouse without fear of no-
toriety. When Little introduced Johnson to the Everleigh sisters,
they were charming but unyielding in allowing Johnson the run of
the place. The color line would not be relaxed, not even for the
world's heavyweight champion. Some sort of compromise was
worked out, so that Belle Schreiber, one of the most desirable companions of the Everleigh Club, left with Johnson and accompanied
him to his hotel room. This introduction to Belle Schreiber and his
consequent long affair with her would prove a near disaster and
very nearly his undoing, for five years later Belle would testify for
the federal government as chief witness in its case against Johnson
for violation of the Mann Act.

Belle never returned to the Everleigh Club. For the next few
years she traveled everywhere with Johnson, introduced by him as
"my wife," though never married to him. She remained with
Johnson until he married Etta Duryea in 1911. She was with him
briefly in Reno in 1910 when he fought Jim Jeffries. When she met
Johnson in Chicago she was twenty-three, tough, beautiful, unin-
hibited, and dangerous. What she saw in Johnson was the chance
to become something more than a mere prostitute; there was the
promise of an exciting life – travel, luxury, and reflected fame.

When Johnson traveled to San Francisco for his match with
Stanley Ketchel, Belle was in tow, a part of the entourage. When
they checked into their hotel, Johnson was surprised to find that
Hattie McLay had preceded them and was waiting for him. Johnson
says Hattie watched the door of his room and lay in wait for him in
the hotel lobby, hoping for reconciliation. "Naturally there was a
state of warfare between Hattie and Belle," Johnson wrote, "which
threatened to break out into the open and disastrous hostilities any

moment."[5] One ruse he said he used to avoid an unwanted meeting with Hattie was to exit his room by means of a rope he let down from a window. But such dodging does not sound like the real Jack Johnson, who sometimes resorted to rough measures in dealing with his women. If the explosion between Belle and Hattie ever happened, it may explain why, after San Francisco, Hattie dropped out of his life forever.

Johnson's fight with Stanley Ketchel took place on October 16, 1909, at Colma, California, just south of San Francisco. Ketchel was middleweight champion, probably the greatest middleweight the world has ever known, with a reputation for being one of the most ferocious fighters in the ring. Johnson outweighed the one hundred sixty pound Ketchel by at least forty pounds, and had the reach on him by several inches. The fight lasted twelve rounds. Ketchel rushed Johnson and fought gamely in every round, and in the eleventh had Johnson on the ropes. In the twelfth he knocked Johnson down. Johnson got to his feet at the count of eight and saw Ketchel rushing at him, eager to finish him. But Johnson got off the first blow, the force of which was increased by Ketchel rushing into it. The blow landed on Ketchel's open mouth, knocking out two of his teeth and ripping Johnson's glove. Ketchel fell to the canvas, out for the count. It was one of the few fights Ketchel ever lost. That same night in Colma, Ketchel and Johnson shot dice together in a friendly game and Ketchel won $700 from Johnson.

When Belle was touring with him, Johnson continued to associate with white prostitutes in Chicago and elsewhere. Belle tolerated them as long as they were temporary, or, in the vernacular, "one-night stands," given nothing more than the standard fee, or a wild ride in one of Johnson's racing cars. But in 1909, shortly after the Stanley Ketchel fight, Johnson met Etta Duryea at a race track in New York, and Belle had a serious rival. Unlike Johnson's other women, Etta was respectable and from a good family with some social position. She had been married and divorced from Clarence Duryea, who ran thoroughbreds at the eastern race tracks. She had been born in Hempstead, Long Island, was twenty-eight when she met Johnson, tall and slender, attractive, with long blond hair. They soon became an item at the track, at night doing the more fashionable clubs in New York City, and it was not long before Johnson began introducing Etta as "my wife." They were not married, however, until January 18, 1911, though Johnson in his autobiography gives the date incorrectly as 1909.[6] What Belle thought of this courtship is not recorded, but it is known that she continued to see Johnson frequently up until the time of his marriage to Etta. His association with and marriage to Etta was another calamity, though neither realized it at the time as such. Etta would not betray Johnson (as Belle later did), yet their marriage would fail because she lacked emotional maturity and could not deal with crises. Johnson's luck with women was running true to form: it was nearly all bad. Shortly before they were married, Etta's father died, and she grew increasingly despondent. She knew of Johnson's secret meetings with Belle and disapproved. No doubt Belle was the cause of arguments between them, which, on one occasion turned violent when Johnson beat Etta so badly she required hospitalization. Feeling remorse, he then showered her with flowers and gifts. Between Etta and Belle he was walking a dangerous tightrope. In Etta he saw respectability and decorum, and in Belle, defiant and a rebel like himself, sensual pleasure.

When Johnson traveled to Philadelphia for his fight with Jack O'Brien in 1909, Etta and Belle accompanied him, though each traveled separately. Belle stayed at one hotel, Etta and Johnson in another. This was Johnson's usual arrangement when he traveled with more than one woman in his entourage. Etta, however, stayed with Johnson in his hotel suite, and was clearly his favorite by choice. Etta learned that Belle was installed in a nearby hotel and at least one argument occurred, but Johnson managed to smooth over the situation. Considering the treatment Etta suffered, it is surprising she agreed to marry Johnson, but she did. In those days inter-racial marriages were not socially acceptable; those who defied convention often became social outcasts. Where Johnson might simply shrug off an overheard remark or printed slur, Etta was easily wounded. Complicating matters for Etta was the world in which Johnson moved, a world inhabited by freeloaders, syco-phants, opportunists, and unsavory characters, those types who are, unfortunately, drawn to the world of boxing. Moreover, marriage did not reform Johnson, and his continued infidelity probably made Etta feel more isolated. All these things proved too much for her to deal with, and in September, 1912, she shot and killed herself. Johnson grieved openly before reporters who shot questions at him the day of the suicide, and before spectators at Etta's grave in Graceland Cemetery, Chicago. His tears were real. Some reporters concluded her suicide was proof that inter-racial marriages, by their very nature, were doomed to failure, and commented upon the "in-compatibility of the races." Only the *Chicago Defender*, a black newspaper with a national circulation, came to Johnson's defense in an effort to tone down the inter-racial aspect.

Much has been written about Johnson's attraction to white women, his fascination for fast automobiles, fast living, and his lifestyle in general. But he was not an easy man to analyze. In some ways he was predictable, and in others, complex. On the subject of white women, Johnson said: "The heartaches which Mary Austin and Clara Kerr had caused me, led me to forswear colored women and to determine that my lot henceforth would be cast only with white women."[7] And to John Lardner he said: "I didn't court white women because I thought I was too good for the others, like they said. It was just that they always treated me better. I never had a colored girl that didn't two-time me."[8] As world champion, Johnson was highly visible, he was newsworthy, and compounding matters, he was unconventional. Whatever he did was magnified in the public mind through the national press. His private life became grist for the mill, presented as a continuing soap opera, and a very controversial one.

Johnson defended himself by saying his romantic affairs were no different than those observed by thousands of other citizens. He admitted these affairs had involved him in scandal, but that imaginative newspaper writers had blown them out of proportion in order to put him in the worst possible light. Johnson, of course, was not without his faults. He had ambivalences and tensions within himself that could ignite to upset his equilibrium. His greatness and decline were both involved in his refusal to accept the status quo, to adjust, temporize, compromise, and "to keep his place."

*   *   *

Jack Johnson believed money was made to be spent. With bills coming due for automobiles, diamonds, furs, and whatever, it was time to make some more money. In 1909, he signed a contract for a vaudeville tour and took Etta with him. She appeared on the boards with him on occasion, though not a regular part of the act, singing a song or giving a recital. Reviews described her performance as stiff and uneasy. But Johnson was always his ebullient self, boxing with a sparring partner, clowning with the medicine ball, dancing the cakewalk, playing the bull fiddle, or joking with the audience. He was a natural performer, always playing to the audience, more entertaining than Jim Jeffries or John L. Sullivan, who usually played character roles in skits especially written for them. Johnson had five inconsequential matches in 1909, three of which were no-decision contests, one knockout, and one by decision. None of his opponents offered a serious challenge. But the purses he won replenished his bank account, as did the money he earned from his vaudeville tour.

Meanwhile, on the national scene, two separate develop-
ments were taking shape that would work their influence on the
sport of boxing, and on Jack Johnson. The first was the contention
that Johnson did not really hold the title of world's heavyweight
champion, that it was a clouded title. A typical example of such
twisted logic was a full-page article that appeared in the *New York
Herald*, July 3, 1910, titled: "The Wanderings of a Championship,"
and mischievously sub-titled: "Story of the Devious and Doubtful
Arrangements by which Jack Johnson Came to Call Himself the
Fistic Monarch." The piece begins with a preamble (incidentally
the article was unsigned) in praise of Jim Jeffries, his winning the
championship from Bob Fitzsimmons, his defense of the title up to
the time of his retirement, and the brilliance of his record. "There
were giants in the land in those days," the preamble says. "Never
within the ken of any man now living will any heavyweight have to
mow through such a field of heavyweights. In these days of bombast
titles and overnight champions any one of the old guard of heavyweight fighters would have been safe in his title for years."[10]
Johnson's title is described as "secondary," "tainted," "cheap," "im-
perfect," and "a title in brevet." It asks the question: "Can a championship be whispered away? Can it pass by word of mouth?" Then
it answers: "To those familiar with the history of the ring and with
its laws there is but one answer. Jeffries is still the heavyweight
champion, as he has been since his defeat of Fitzsimmons." As with
all arguments on this particular subject, it begins with the premise
that the fight between Marvin Hart and Jack Root, in Reno,
Nevada, July 3, 1905 (in which the referee was Jim Jeffries) was not
a fight for the world's heavyweight championship at all. But rather
it was advertised as such in order to insure a profitable gate, and
that Jeffries would formally pass the title to the winner of the fight.
"No word was ever heard from Jeffries himself with regard to this
arrangement," the piece continues, "so far as the public knows. The

announcement certainly lent to the fight an importance it could not otherwise have had, as neither Hart nor Root ranked high in ring history. At the conclusion of the fight, marked by a knockout, it was announced from the ringside that Jeffries had hailed Hart the heavyweight champion by virtue of his own retirement from the ring." To further bolster its contention, the piece quotes a contradictory statement by Jeffries which says he refused to present the title to the winner – "Nobody can give away championships."

> *Here therefore started this championship title which Johnson claims. It is tainted at the source, first by Jeffries' denial that he ever entered into any such arrangement as that announced to the public and second by reason of the fact as stated by Jeffries, that "nobody can give away championships." They must be earned. That Root-Hart fight was of slight moment in those days and the flimsy, fly-blown title claimed by Hart gained him title.*[11]

The writer does not say that Jeffries by his mere presence at the Hart-Root fight in Reno, in his capacity as referee, countenanced the whole affair. Nor does it say that the title was not considered clouded for the brief time Hart held it, nor was it clouded or "tainted" during the three years Tommy Burns held it, before losing it to Jack Johnson. It was only *after* Johnson won the title that the argument was advanced and the notion put forth that Jeffries was still the world champion. The piece is more than mischievous when it refers to Johnson's pursuit of Tommy Burns around the world for a match when it says: "For two years Jack Johnson had been chasing Burns all over the country in an effort to have a try at the title which Burns carried and for which Johnson yearned as he would have yearned for a watermelon or a fried chicken."[12] Of course, there was another motive for advancing the argument of the clouded title. Put simply, it was to coax Jim Jeffries out of retirement and into a match with Jack Johnson that would decide once and for all who was world champion. Johnson had this to say about the matter:

> It was virtually necessary for me to wage two ring battles before I established undisputed claim to the championship. My fight with Burns really gave me the title, for he was the recognized champion. When I acquired his laurels, the question suddenly arose as to whether or not Burns was the champion. It was stoutly declared by some that Jeffries was the champion, because he actually had not lost the title in the ring, merely having voluntarily relinquished it to Hart, who had been defeated by Burns. It was upon this basis that Burns claimed the championship, and it was never questioned until I established my claim. At any rate I was not permitted to rest secure in the title. I was constantly harassed and criticized. Those who conceded, but resented my rightful claim to the title, started a turmoil by hunting a "white hope" or one who would regain the title for the white race.[13]

The second development was the search for the "white hope," which caught the fancy of the sporting world and would continue to do so for the next six years. Jack London is usually credited with coining the phrase "white hope" after the Burns-Johnson fight in Sydney, Australia, though he did not use those exact words. In any event, the search was on for a contender who might defeat Johnson, and there were many hopefuls. It seemed that anyone who had ever entered a ring who was over six feet tall and weighed over two hundred pounds was considered a hopeful if he was white. Actually, some of the best contenders were black boxers, such as Sam Langford, Sam McVey, and Joe Jeanette, but Johnson had already met and defeated them. While the inconsequential opponents Johnson fought in 1909 may have been advertised as white hopes, none of them really offered Johnson much of a challenge.

One young boxer who did offer considerable promise was Luther McCarty, from Nebraska, who stood six feet four and weighed two hundred and ten pounds, and who may have been the best fighter among all the white hopes. His rise was meteoric; in quick succession he knocked out Al Kaufmann, Jim Flynn, and Al Palzer. But he would never meet Jack Johnson. He died of a brain hemorrhage during a fight in Canada, which may have been caused by an injury a few days before when he had fallen from a horse. Jess Willard, known as the Pottawatomie Giant, was the biggest man in the ring in 1909. He was six feet six inches tall, a reach of eighty-three inches, and weighed two hundred and fifty pounds. At this stage, however, he was a rank amateur with little ring experience. In a fight with Joe Cox in Springfield, Missouri, Willard grabbed the referee and used him as a shield against Cox's punches, and was hooted by spectators. Willard's manager was so disgusted with his performance that he dropped him on the spot.[14]

The choice had narrowed down to one man – Jim Jeffries – who, in the minds of many, was still champion. He had retired undefeated, and in his retirement his legend had grown. He seemed the best of all the white hopes: he was tough, he could hit, he was as big as a bear, he had endurance, and he was the only boxer that could make Jack Johnson extend himself. The problem with this assessment was that it was based on the Jim Jeffries of an earlier day, when he had been at the peak of his career. In the six years since his retirement, Jeffries had spent more time at his saloon and restaurant in Los Angeles acting as host than he had working on his alfalfa farm. Customers often insisted on buying the famous fighter a beer and dinner. He had, indeed, grown to the proportions of a bear, and weighed almost three hundred pounds. He had not entered the ring in six years, and he was thirty-five years old.

When talk about a match between Jefferies and Johnson first began to circulate, a story told by Jeffries caught the imagination of sports fans everywhere. According to the story, Jeffries was in a saloon in San Francisco when, of all people, Jack Johnson happened to walk in and asked Jeffries when they were going to fight. "Right now, if you like," Jeffries replied. Jeffries pulled out a large roll of bills, put them on the bar, and said, "This is for the hospital expenses. You match that amount. We'll go down to the cellar, lock the door, fight it out, and the man who leaves the cellar on his own feet can pick up the money here on the bar." "But I don't want to fight in a locked cellar," Johnson said. "I want to fight before the public." Jeffries seemed to think it was a good way to stop Johnson from pestering him for a fight, and a good joke on Johnson, who turned on his heel and left the saloon.[15] The story may or may not be true. It sounds like the concoction of a sports writer, but since it has been repeated so frequently it may actually have happened, if not exactly as Jeffries told it.

Jeffries was a man who often contradicted himself. When he was first asked by sports writers if he would fight Johnson, he said "I will never go back into the ring."[16] But as pressure mounted for him to carry the banner of the best white hope, he began to equivocate. Early in 1909, Jeffries went on a nationwide vaudeville tour, beginning in San Francisco and ending in New York, with boxing exhibitions as part of the show, and sports writers took note of this, and urged him to come out of retirement. Jeffries, however, had doubts about his condition. He would have to lose seventy or eighty pounds, and he would have to train hard for many months to get into proper condition. Was it worth the effort?

I did not want to return to the ring. I had been idle, as far as boxing went, for six years, and for practically a year before that I had not fought one serious match. For almost five years I scarcely had touched a boxing glove except to spar for fun, or for some charity. I had worked lightly on the stage for thirteen weeks.[17]

In New York, Jeffries met Tex Rickard and was persuaded to sign an agreement to fight Jack Johnson. Jeffries wrote that he did not take the agreement seriously, as it was filled with escape clauses that left him free to cancel if he found he could not get into fighting trim. Some writers have speculated that Jeffries signed the agreement because he was broke. This is not true. He had an adequate income from his saloon and restaurant business, he had made money dabbling in Los Angeles real estate, and had earned fifty thousand dollars from his latest vaudeville contract. Three weeks after signing the agreement, he sailed for Europe, where he checked in at the famous watering hole and clinic at Carlsbad, Germany. There he consulted doctors to learn whether his condition was such that he might safely lose the necessary weight, and whether his body was equal to the rigors of hard training to put him in the best fighting condition. While at Carlsbad, he took baths in the hot springs to lose weight, and began a program of roadwork. He returned a month later, still undecided on the match with Johnson, and set out on another vaudeville tour that lasted thirteen weeks, which earned him eighty thousand dollars. The public thought his stay at Carlsbad had marked the beginning of training, and some were puzzled by his return to vaudeville. The clamor for Jeffries to meet Johnson grew louder and louder, and whether Jeffries was willing to accept it or not, the public had chosen him as the white hope.

One day in 1909, Jeffries asked his old manager, De Witt Van Cort, what he thought of the talk about a Johnson fight. "You'd be crazy to listen," Van Cort replied. "You have nothing to gain and everything to lose. If you beat him everyone will say he is no good and never could fight, and if you lose everyone will say you were crazy to fight. It may be another case of old John L. if you do."[18] John L. Sullivan had been a hero to Jeffries from his boyhood, the greatest fighter of them all, a grand old man, the last of the bare-knuckled boxers. Few things in his life had troubled him as much as the memory of Sullivan, old and fat, out of condition, being battered helpless by a fast, younger man.[19]

The Long Road to Reno

Jeffries left for his training camp at Rowadennan, near the town of Ben Lomond, in the Santa Cruz Mountains of California His training crew consisted of his brother Jack, Bob Armstrong, Joe Choynski, James Corbett, and his manager, Sam Berger. In the early stages of his training he was not able to do much roadwork, he tired easily, a condition he regarded as temporary, due to his six year retirement from the ring. The effort required to get into condition was enormous; he had to scale down to two hundred and twenty pounds. He became grouchy and withdrawn. Reporters who visited his training camp seldom saw him, and if they did, described him as touchy as a grizzly bear. His training crew, especially James Corbett, drew a protective ring about him, shielding him from unwanted visitors. Probably he had second thoughts about his agreement with Tex Rickard when he wrote: "I had permitted myself to be lured into a fight I did not want because I was too good-natured to say no, and had given a half-promise in spite of the advice of my best friends."[1]

But he trained hard, and after eight weeks he could run ten

miles on the road, box ten to twelve rounds without pause against his sparring partners, and work long stretches punching the bags. Even so, he knew he was not the man he had been six years before, but he was gaining strength and endurance, and if he peaked at the right moment he might be good enough to beat Johnson. One day Tex Rickard appeared at the training camp to see for himself if Jeffries would be in condition for the fight, and he was pleased with what he saw. Jeffries sparred with his brother Jack for several rounds. Rickard thought it a fine performance. Jeffries looked powerful. He had lost much of the fat, his shoulders and torso were huge, muscles rippled over his chest and biceps. Sports writers took the line that Jeffries was again his old self, still the champion, and that he was equal to the role of white hope. Jeffries received hundreds of letters from fans across the nation, urging him to restore honor to the white race, and to smash once and for all Jack Johnson's golden smile. Jeffries may have been flattered by all the attention, and perhaps he began to believe that he really could beat Johnson.

In December, 1909, Jeffries left California for New York City, accompanied by his manager, Sam Berger. The leading boxing promoters would be there to bid for the fight – now publicized as "The Fight of the Century." Sam Berger would negotiate for Jeffries, and George Little and Sig Hart for Jack Johnson. Among the promoters were "Tuxedo Eddie" Graney, who hoped to book the fight for the Tuxedo Boxing Club of San Francisco. Another San Francisco promoter, "Sunny Jim" Coffroth was represented by Jack Gleason, and it was hinted in the press they had Jeffries under contract. Then there was Tom McCarey, who hoped to win the fight for the Pacific Club in Los Angeles. Phil King represented Hugh McIntosh, who had promoted the Tommy Burns-Jack Johnson fight in Sydney, who wanted the fight held in Australia. And finally there was George Lewis "Tex" Rickard, who was regarded in boxing circles as a newcomer and novice.

Rickard had promoted the Joe Gans-Battling Nelson fight in Goldfield, Nevada, September 1906. That event had attracted nationwide interest and focused attention on the new mining metropolis of Goldfield. Rickard's success was regarded in the boxing world as a fluke, and he was not considered a serious rival. Rickard had worked as a cowboy in Texas, later as a frontier marshal. He had joined the Alaska gold rush, managed a saloon in Nome, then drifted back to the States. Drawn by the promise of adventure and wealth, he joined the rush to Goldfield, the greatest boomtown in Nevada since the days of Virginia City. He opened his Northern Saloon, soon to become famous all over Nevada, which prospered with the growth of Goldfield, especially its gambling casino. He built a fine house in Goldfield and his name became familiar to everyone in Nevada. Rickard's competitors for the Johnson-Jeffries fight had thought he lacked enough money to win the prize. But they were in for a surprise. Rickard had the backing of Thomas F. Cole, a Minnesota capitalist who owned gold and silver mines in Alaska and Nevada. Rickard had acted as Cole's agent in Nevada, buying for him large blocks of stock in the most productive mines.

The bids were to be opened in the grand ballroom of the Hotel Albany in New York City, with the press in full attendance. However, the day before the bids were to be opened, New York City District Attorney William T. Jerome announced that because boxing was illegal in New York anyone associated with the bidding process would be arrested and jailed. Jerome may have been grandstanding for publicity but he meant what he said. His reasoning – which seemed stretched to the point of credulity by many – was that since boxing was illegal in the state of New York it was also illegal for promoters to bid for a fight in that state, even if the fight itself was to be held across the continent, or, should McIntosh win the bidding, on another continent. When the bidders recovered from their surprise at Jerome's ultimatum, it was decided to move the proceedings to Meyer's Hotel in Hoboken, New Jersey, outside of Jerome's jurisdiction. The party traveled by ferryboat across the Hudson River, followed by a small army of sports writers. The first bid opened was from "Tuxedo Eddie" Graney, who offered a $70,000 guarantee, plus all the motion picture rights. Jack Gleason and James Coffroth offered a $125,000 guarantee with no motion picture rights. Hugh McIntosh, the Australian promoter, offered $100,000 and one-fourth of the motion picture rights – but only if the fight were held in Australia. Each promoter had enclosed a certified check for $5,000 with his bid. When Rickard's bid was opened, a certified check for $5,000 fell out of the envelope, and fifteen $1,000 bills. In addition, Rickard had pledged to Johnson and Jeffries $10,000 in cash if his bid were accepted. Rickard's bid was for $101,000 with sixty-six and two-thirds percent of the motion picture rights, with the fight to be held in California, Nevada, or Utah. Tom McCarey's bid was opened last. It guaranteed a purse of $110,000 and fifty percent of the picture rights. Rickard's bid had the edge, enhanced by the display of $1,000 bills, and everyone knew it. Johnson had already indicated he favored it. But it was agreed to let the matter rest overnight. The winning bid would be announced to the press on the following morning. When the moment came, with the ballroom filled to capacity, everyone present considered it a foregone conclusion that Rickard had won the bidding, and they were right.[2]

The fight was scheduled for the Fourth of July, 1910. That would allow ample time for training, publicity, reams of copy to be written by sports writers, wrangling between fighters and managers, unexpected surprises, or whatever. One of the first rumors to make the rounds (no one seemed to know where it had originated) said that the fight was fixed. Johnson had agreed to lay down for a huge sum so that Jeffries might reclaim his championship, or to put a spin on it, Jeffries had agreed to lay down so that Johnson might keep his championship. Neither rumor had any truth to it. But rumors die hard, and talk of a crooked fight persisted until almost the day of the match.

Though the fight was six months distant in the future, sports writers began turning out copy on the upcoming event. Jeffries had returned to the seclusion of his training camp at Rowadennan, and James Corbett, who seemed to have appointed himself chief factotum of Rowadennan, barred entry to most reporters. Jack Johnson was first on the west coast, then in Chicago, and his movements were tracked by the press, especially his frequent traffic violations for speeding. He had not yet selected a site for his training camp. There was precious little news for the sports writers to base any stories on. So they dug into the files and rewrote stories of past fights of both boxers. When they had exhausted that vein, old interviews with the two fighters were reprinted. If they couldn't approach either Jeffries or Johnson, they sought out comments from Tex Rickard, Sam Berger, George Little, and the talkative James Corbett, who was always ready with a pointed remark. Finally, there was the field of speculation to write about, and some sports writers wondered aloud (in print) if the fight was fixed.

These rumors eventually caught the attention of social reformers, who had been waging a fairly successful campaign to have prize fighting declared illegal in all states. To understand the antagonism of social reformers toward boxing it is helpful to realize that the movement was basically composed of Puritans and Progressives in rebellion against what they saw as demoralizing and uncivilized influences detrimental to the American character. Their spirit was puritanical, militant, and often belligerent. They were especially well-organized in the large Midwestern cities where they displayed their power in large parades and vigilante-type raids on saloons.[3] But they also had chapters and affiliates in many large eastern cities. Some of these organizations, such as the Anti-Saloon League,

Women's Christian Temperance Union, Law and Order League, The Committee for Public Decency, and others, worked to force their opinions on others by forming pressure groups to work for legislated morality. Many of these organizations were headed by ministers and church auxiliaries. They were opposed to liquor, gambling, prostitution, tobacco, prize fighting – not necessarily in that order – and in 1919 achieved their greatest victory with the passage of Prohibition. Underlying the reform movement was a definite xenophobia, or fear of immigrants who were coming into the country in great numbers. These new immigrants – including semi-literate Russian Jews, Irish Catholics, Italians, Polish, and others – were seen as the very people most likely to fall victim to the evils of liquor, gambling, prostitution, and prize fighting.[4] There was also the widespread fear that these immigrants, eager to find employment at any price and who might be willing to work for lower wages, were a threat to any Anglo-Saxon who had a job. And so the social reformers had mixed feelings about equality. That attitude extended to blacks, who had been kept in economic peonage, if not through legislation, then through social and economic conformity.

The rumors that the fight was fixed simply confirmed their belief that prize fighting was not only uncivilized but synonymous with gambling, and therefore a vice. There was also the person of Jack Johnson. He represented everything the reformers hated. He was a professional boxer, he kept prostitutes, he liked to gamble, he smoked cigars, drank liquor (actually he sipped champagne through a straw), and made no public apologies for his actions. He was perceived by reformers as one who openly flaunted his vices before the public. He was arrogant, lascivious, and the devil incarnate. But what bothered the reformers most about the Johnson-Jeffries fight was the problem of race, though they never described it as such. To them it was not simply another prize fight. It was a contest for racial superiority, and Jim Jeffries was the white hope. The whole idea of the fight – and the fact that Johnson held the title of world heavy-weight champion – acknowledged a kind of equality, that a black man had the opportunity to rise to the top, at least in one profession. One black journalist realized this and was critical of social reformers for trying to stop the fight. "Just because the Negro has an equal chance, that in itself, in their opinion, is enough to constitute a national disgrace." And he went on to say that he hoped Johnson would win and give Jeffries a good thrashing "just to make it a good national disgrace."[5] One prominent black minister, Rev. Reverdy C. Ransom, of the Bethel African Methodist Church in New York City, attempted to defuse the race issue when he said: "No respectable colored minister in the United States is interested in the pugilistic contest between Johnson and Jeffries from the standpoint of race. We do not think Jack Johnson thinks or has ever thought of holding the championship for the 'black race.' Johnson is not trying to win the Negro championship, but to hold and defend his title against all comers, regardless of race or color."[6]

But not all black people were supportive of Johnson. Booker T. Washington, in a speech given to the Detroit Young Men's Christian Association said: "Jack Johnson has harmed rather than helped the race. I wish to say emphatically that his actions do not meet my approval, and I'm sure they do not meet with the approval of the colored race."[7] Emmett Jay Scott, who was Washington's personal secretary, had remarked in 1909 that Jack Johnson needed to be more humble in public, more ingratiating with the press.[8] E. L. Blackshear, who was president of the State Normal and Industrial College in Prairie View, Texas, and a leader in the black education movement, said that should Johnson win over Jeffries "the anti-Negro sentiment will quickly and dangerously collect itself ready to strike back at any undue exhibitions of rejoicing on the part of Negroes."[9] Booker T. Washington believed that equality could be achieved through patience, persuasion, and education. Booker T.

Washington might be invited to the White House for lunch, but Jack Johnson, never.

Meanwhile, it seemed to everyone that Tex Rickard had found in San Francisco the perfect place for the world's heavyweight championship match. There were assurances from "Sunny Jim" Cofforth, political boss of San Francisco, and San Francisco Mayor Edward H. McCarthy, that the fight would go on as scheduled. While Governor James C. Gillett had made no direct statement concerning the match, he had given implied approval through remarks leaked to the press. Reports from Rowadennan said Jeffries ran fifteen miles every day and was mean as a bear. His sparring partners were said to be battered and bruised by the big fellow's gloves. Actually, Jeffries spent more time trout fishing on the nearby San Lorenzo River than he did sparring in the ring. Such hyperbole was characteristic of James Corbett, who had begun a campaign of psychological warfare against the Johnson camp. "Take it from me," Corbett told newspapermen gathered at the front gate to Rowadennan, "the black boy has a yellow streak, and Jeff will bring it out when he gets him into that ring."[10] Johnson, of course, was not in the least disturbed by these remarks. In April, 1910, he set up his training camp at Seal Beach, near San Francisco. Other than an occasional sparring match, he did little training in April. He preferred to drive his fast cars along the beach or into the mountains. He was sometimes seen sunning himself at the beach or swimming in the surf. Never shy of publicity, he willingly gave interviews to reporters, tossing the medicine ball from one hand to the other as he spoke, or playing the bull fiddle for their amusement. Other days the camp would be less casual, when an argument between Johnson and his manager, George Little, would suddenly erupt, and observers sensed tension was building between the two men.

Tex Rickard had selected an empty lot at the corner of Market and Sixth streets for his arena. It would seat thirty thousand spectators and cost $35,000 to build. Tons of lumber appeared on the site in early May, and by the end of the month the frame of the big stadium was taking shape. Meanwhile, the social reformers had launched their campaign to stop the fight. As letters, post cards, telegrams, and telephone messages protesting the fight increased in volume, Governor Gillett tried to appease the reformers by referring to the match as a "sparring contest," which was allowed under California law.[11] This euphemism was seen as mere subterfuge by reformers and enraged them all the more. In Cincinnati, Ohio, a Mr. George Rockwell, who had put together a national coalition of business and church people, had printed one million post cards with the message: "STOP THE FIGHT. THIS IS THE 20TH CENTURY." Printed with Governor Gillett's name and address ready for mailing, they were distributed to the faithful. The Governor's office was swamped with mail.[12] One late afternoon, as the Governor left the capitol building, he was confronted by the spectacle of fifty ministers kneeling in a prayer circle on the marble steps, praying for both divine and gubernatorial intervention to stop the fight.[13]

Tex Rickard was so sure the fight would come off in San Francisco that he saw the protests as good free publicity. But Rickard had underestimated the power of the reformers. The first hint that Governor Gillett might be wavering came from "Tad," the talented *San Francisco Examiner* cartoonist and sports writer, whose real name was T. A. Dorgan, when he wrote on June 15: "There is a wild rumor that Governor Gillett has wired District Attorney Fickert to stop the fight. But the latter laughs at the idea."[14] When the reformers saw that protests and demonstrations were not forceful enough, they turned to political intervention. They had a powerful ally in U. S. Congressman William S. Bennett of New York, who was chairman of the House Committee on Foreign Relations. Bennett sent a telegram to the San Francisco Board of Trade stating that the upcoming fight and the controversy surrounding it jeopardized San Francisco's chances of becoming the site for the Panama-Pacific Exposition. Congressman Bennett did not explain how the fight could possibly have any bearing on the Exposition (which did not occur until five years later, in 1915) other than the matter of site selection. But the intimidation worked. Governor Gillett panicked and ordered the Attorney General to stop the fight. Gillett was quoted as saying: "Tell Tex Rickard to get out of my state. Tell him to take Johnson and Jeffries with him. What he is planning is a prize fight and against the law."[15] San Francisco Mayor Edward McCarthy was in the east when Gillett's announcement was made. He told reporters as he boarded the train for San Francisco: "I am running San Francisco. I am taking no orders from Gillett or his Attorney General. You can bet your last dollar the big fight will be pulled off in my town just as advertised."[16] But in speaking these words Mayor McCarthy may not have realized that the movement to stop the fight could be traced back to Washington, D.C. He made a trip to Sacramento to try and persuade the Governor to change his mind, but Gillett was unyielding. Gillett said if the fight took place the state militia would be called out to stop it.[17] The Governor came in for some criticism for his decision, most notably from Jack London, who wrote: "A Governor of a State whose function is to execute the law arrogated to itself the function of interpreting the law – a function that peculiarly and specifically belongs to the courts. Failing in getting an injunction from the courts, the Governor enforced his decree by calling for troops. Every man who applauded this action applauded, consciously or unconsciously, a foul blow. Had such persons had a training in the brutal fair play of the ring they would have been fairer minded than to applaud the consummation they devoutly wished, but a consummation achieved in any way except devoutly."[18] The reformers, of course, rejoiced. At this point they believed they had stopped the fight. Governor Gillett received messages of praise from

James Jeffries and Bob Fitzsimmons touch gloves before their championship fight at the Coney Island Athletic Club, near Brooklyn, on June 9, 1899. The fight lasted eleven rounds, Fitzsimmons winning most of the early rounds on points with his superior speed and footwork. But he could not hurt Jeffries. Fitzsimmons was knocked to the canvas in the 9th and 10th rounds. In the 11th Jeffries hit him with a left and a right to the jaw, knocking out Fitzsimmons. *Brooklyn Public Library, Brooklyn Collection*

Jack Johnson arriving at Vancouver, B.C. after his fight in Australia with Tommy Burns. *Author's collection*

James Jeffries at Rowadennan, his training camp near Ben Lomond, California, in the Santa Cruz Mountains. Jeffries, dressed in hunting clothes, poses with his dog. Jeffries also enjoyed trout fishing on the nearby San Lorenza River. *Paul Elcano Collection*

Tex Rickard built this brick home in Goldfield with profits from his famous "Northern," Goldfield's most prominent saloon and gambling hall. Rickard also made a small fortune buying and selling stocks in Nevada gold mines. *Author's collection*

Jack Dempsey (at left) and Johnny Sudenberg face-off before their 1915 fight at Goldfield, Nevada. At this time Dempsey was a green, inexperienced boxer and worked as a miner in the Goldfield-Tonopah mines. A few weeks later, the two men would fight again in Tonopah, a fight which Dempsey described as "one of my hardest. I don't remember any fight I ever engaged in which I was forced to extend myself more." *Author's collection*

Advertising post card issued for the Joe Gans-Kid Herman fight at Tonopah, Nevada, January 1, 1907. *Paul Elcano Collection*

Stanley Ketchel and Jack Johnson pose for the photographer before their historic fight at Colma, California, on October 16, 1909. The fight lasted twelve rounds, Johnson winning by a knockout. Ketchel was middleweight champion and Johnson outweighed him by at least forty pounds. But Ketchel knocked Johnson to the canvas in the twelfth round, putting up a game fight. *Chicago Historical Society*

"Signing of the articles of The Jeffries-Johnson Contest over a case of Pommery," Hoboken, New Jersey, October 29, 1909. Pictured are George Considine, Abe Attel, Bob Vernon, Jack Johnson, George Little, James Jeffries, Sam Berger and Bob Murphy. Photograph by Fred Hemment. *Rick Reviglio Collection*

The Hotel Golden, headquarters for the sporting crowd that gathered in Reno for the fight. Among the celebrities who stayed here during fight week were John L. Sullivan, Bob Fitzsimmons, Jack London, Rex Beach, Bat Masterson, and others. To accommodate the influx of fans, the Golden did a bit of improvisation and set up sleeping cots in the lobby and dining room each night at midnight. *Gil Schmidtmann collection*

Sport fans arriving by train at the station in Reno, Nevada for the Johnson-Jeffries fight. *Nevada Historical Society*

A portion of the crowd gathered at the railroad station in Reno to greet James Jeffries upon his arrival. Jeffries, who shied away from such demonstrations, slipped off the rear of the train and was whisked off in an automobile to Moana Springs, his training camp. *Paul Elcano Collection*

Headquarters for Jack Johnson fans was the Johnson Club, normally a saloon and bean-ery, which offered Buffalo Beer, hamburgers for 10¢, a bowl of chili for 10¢, hot cakes and coffee for 10¢. A few doors down the street was the headquarters for the Jeffries Club. *Gil Schmidtmann collection*

Rick's Resort, three miles outside Reno on the Lawton Springs road, was Johnson's training camp and residence before the fight. Johnson and his party occupied the entire second floor. *Gil Schmidtmann collection*

Jack Johnson (right) poses with sparring partner Al Kaufman (left) at Rick's Resort outside Reno. At far left, next to the man in the striped shirt and bow-tie, stands George Cotton, another of Johnson's sparring partners. The man at left wearing a hat with a towel draped over his shoulder is Sig Hart, Johnson's manager at the time. *Paul Elcano Collection*

Jack Johnson and a sparring partner at his training camp at Rick's Resort, outside Reno. *Paul Elcano Collection*

A large crowd watches Jack Johnson sparring with a partner at Rick's Resort (in background). This photograph was taken when Governor Denver Dickerson paid a visit to Johnson's training quarters, accompanied by Tex Rickard and John L. Sullivan. *Paul Elcano Collection*

"Johnson and Cotton." George Cotton was an accomplished boxer in his own right. Cotton said of Johnson: "Johnson is the great-est boxer that ever pulled on a glove. It is next to impossible to hit him." *Paul Elcano Collection*

Jack Johnson and Al Kaufman sparring at Rick's Resort. Johnson trained hard for the fight, sparring with partners every day. *Paul Elcano Collection*

From left to right: George Cotton, Doc Furey, Jack Johnson, and Al Kaufman. This photograph was taken at Rick's Resort a few days before the fight. *Gil Schmidtmann collection*

James Jeffries meets Nevada Governor Denver Dickerson at his Moana Springs training camp. Tex Rickard is at center of view. Governor Dickerson's visit to Moana Springs gave Jeffries' fans a rare opportunity to see him spar with partners in the ring.
Paul Elcano Collection

Jim Jeffries working out on the bag platform at Moana Springs as crowd watches. *Gil Schmidtmann collection*

Jim Jeffries (center) on the porch of his cottage at Moana Springs. The man at far right is Tex Rickard. *Gil Schmidtmann collection*

Jim Jeffries welcomed Tex Rickard to his cottage at Moana Springs. In the background between the two men, "Gentleman" Jim Corbett watches the exchange of greetings. *Gil Schmidtmann collection*

Dressed in his fishing clothes and holding a flyrod, Jeffries shakes hands with a well-wisher. Standing next to Jeffries, wearing a cap, is John L. Sullivan.
Gil Schmidtmann collection

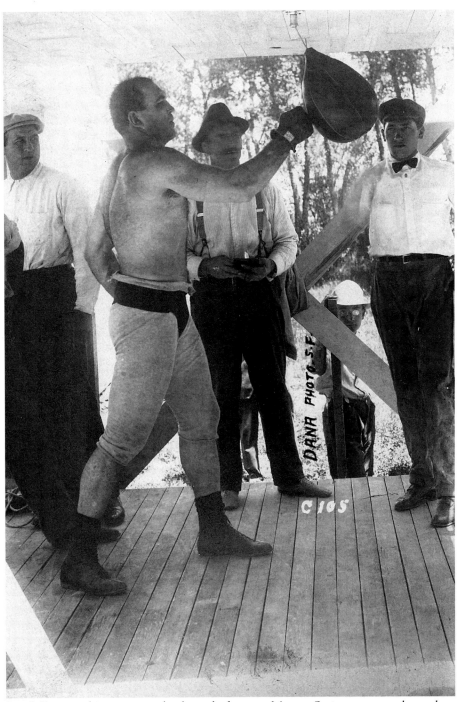

Jim Jeffries working out on the bag platform at Moana Springs as crowd watches.
Gil Schmidtmann collection

No.35. Gleason, Tommy Burns, McIntosh, Sullivan, Gotch, Fitz, Sharkey.

Jeffries shakes hands with John L. Sullivan. From left to right: Gleason, Tommy Burns, McIntosh, Sullivan, Frank Gotch, Bob Fitzsimmons, and Tom Sharkey. *Paul Elcano Collection*

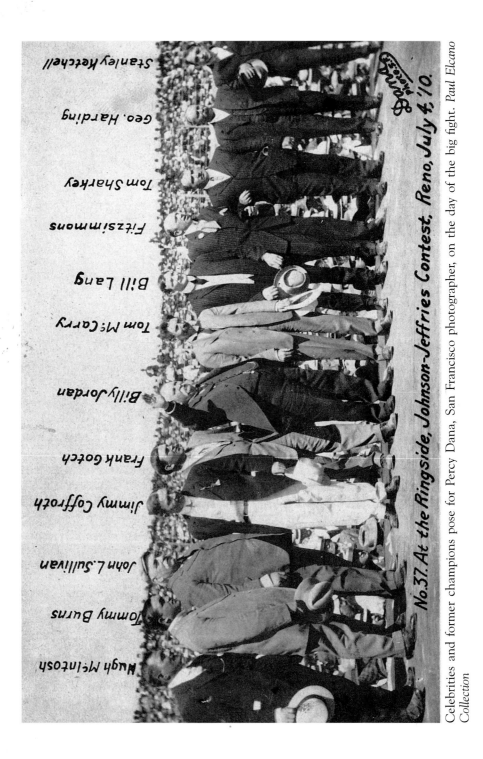

Hugh McIntosh Tommy Burns John L. Sullivan Jimmy Coffroth Frank Gotch Billy Jordan Tom McCarry Bill Lang Fitzsimmons Tom Sharkey Geo. Harding Stanley Hetchell

No.37. At the Ringside, Johnson-Jeffries Contest, Reno, July 4, '10.

Celebrities and former champions pose for Percy Dana, San Francisco photographer, on the day of the big fight. *Paul Elcano Collection*

Jeffries   Tex Rickard   July 4 • 1910   Johnson

Dana Photo S.F.

A composite photograph created by photographer Dana to publicize the fight. Tex Rickard, dressed in a three-piece suit, shirt and tie, in center of picture. *Paul Elcano Collection*

A sea of faces inside the arena, as photographed by San Francisco photographer Percy Dana. *Paul Elcano Collection*

Section A of the arena, filled with spectators awaiting the fight. Tex Rickard hired 175 men working ten hours a day to complete the arena in only thirteen days. *Author's collection*

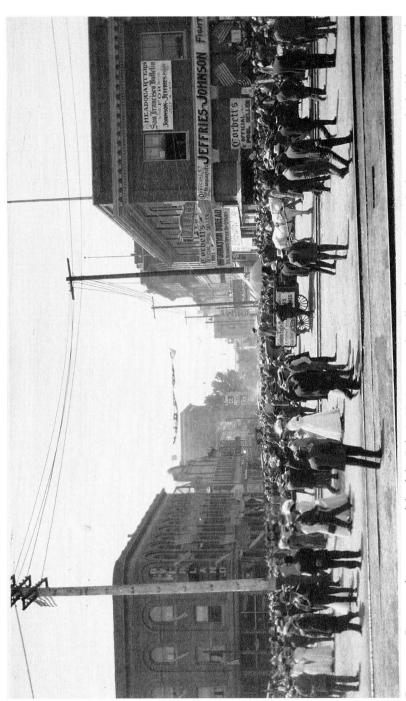

Downtown Reno on the morning of the fight, July 4, 1910, as crowds walk to the arena. Note the banners on the building at right promoting the event, and a sign for "Corbett's Official Book," which was the largest betting office in Reno. *Paul Elcano Collection*

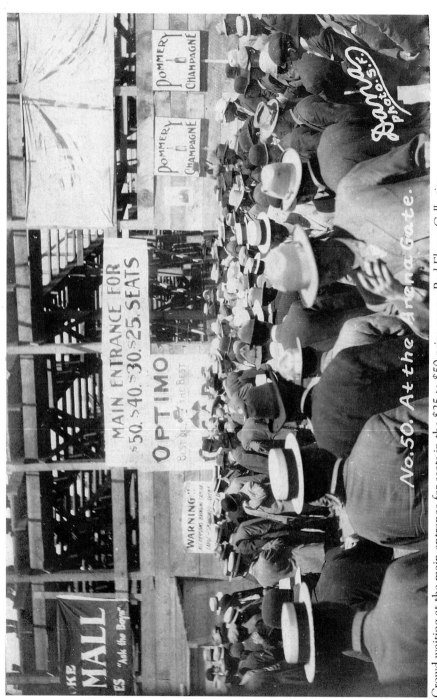

Crowd waiting at the main entrance for seats in the $25 to $50 price range. *Paul Elcano Collection*

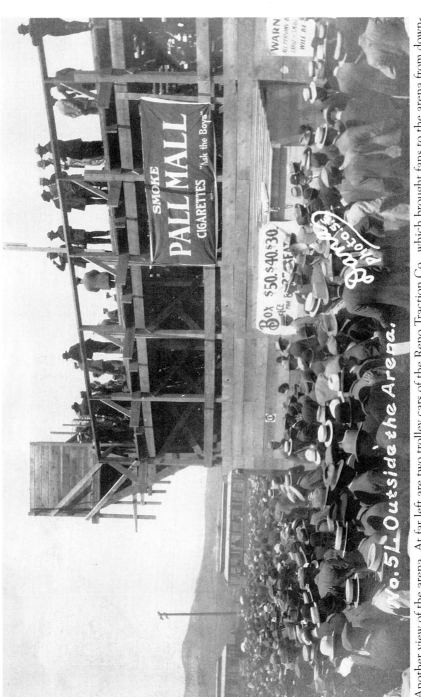

No. 51. Outside the Arena.

Another view of the arena. At far left are two trolley cars of the Reno Traction Co., which brought fans to the arena from downtown. At bottom right is a portion of a sign headed "Warning," which said that anyone carrying a firearm would not be admitted. Liquor was also prohibited inside the arena. *Paul Elcano Collection*

No. 63. The Crowd at the Ringside. Reno, July 4.

DANA Photo S.F.

'BULL DURHAM

COPYRIGHT BY

A panoramic view of the ring and part of the arena. The crowd was estimated at 19,000. *Paul Elcano Collection*

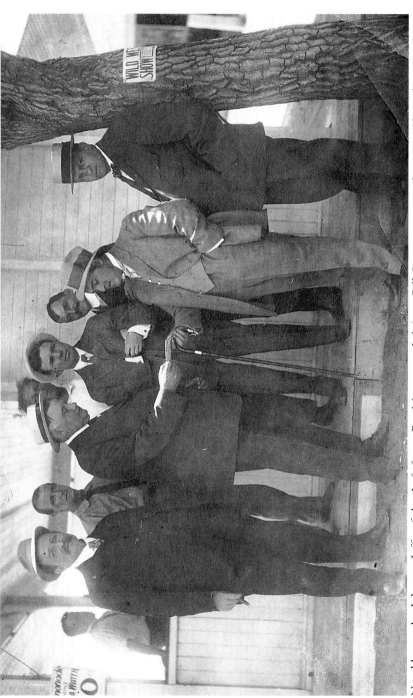

Notables at the Johnson-Jeffies fight. Left front: Bat Masterson; center, obsc.: Joe Cheynski; right front: Hugo Kelly; right rear: Hugh McIntosh. Also: Battling Nelson and Tommy Burns. *Nevada Historical Society*

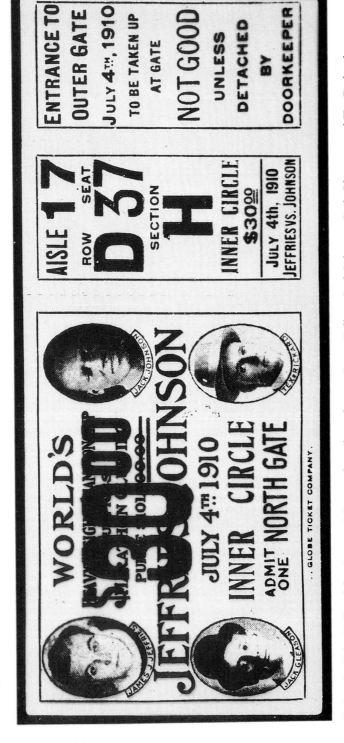

Ticket for "The Fight of the Century." Pictured on the ticket are James Jeffries, Jack Johnson, Jack Gleason, and Tex Rickard.
Paul Elcano Collection

Crowd going to Jefferies and Johnson fight. RenoNev. 4-7-10

"Crowd going to Jeffries and Johnson fight. Reno, Nev." The arena is at center right. Fans came in automobiles, buggies, on horseback, or walked. Note the long lines of people waiting to enter the arena. *Paul Elcano Collection*

No.36. Gleason, Sullivan, McIntosh, Gotch, Fitz, Sharkey.

From left to right: Gleason, Sullivan, McIntosh, Gotch, Fitzsimmons, and Sharkey. *Paul Elcano Collection*

Cartoon strip illustrating the favorite punches of the two contestants – Jeffries executing a kidney punch and a left to the mid-section, and Johnson connecting with a right uppercut. *Author's collection*

Racist cartoon depicting Jack Johnson as a fun-loving simpleton. *Author's collection*

all over the nation. The *San Francisco Chronicle* wrote that the Governor's desk was almost buried beneath the weight of the messages.[19] The Rev. George Burlingame, pastor of the First Baptist Church in Oakland, said the action of the Governor put him in the same company with Abraham Lincoln.[20]

Tex Rickard did not think so. If there were no fight, he faced financial ruin. He had already spent a considerable sum on the stadium, permits, the cash advances made to Johnson and Jeffries, and other expenses. There was also the matter of advance ticket sales. Either he had to honor them or refund the money. He considered personally suing Governor Gillett, but when the Governor heard of this he replied testily: "If Tex Rickard is looking for a fight with me he will get a bigger one than he has advertised for the Fourth of July. We've had enough of prize fights and prize fight promoters. They've been breaking the law long enough and we'll have no more of it. When the fighters lick the State of California they can go ahead and lick each other, but not before."[21]

Jeffries was trout fishing near his camp at Rowadennan when someone brought him the news. His first response was disbelief, then disgust. The next day Rickard came to the camp and talked with Jeffries. Rickard said he was considering moving the fight to Nevada, the only state in which prize fighting was legal. He mentioned Salt Lake City as a possibility, but in Utah a fight required a special permit by the Legislature and Governor. Remembering his experience with California politicians, he decided against it. Rickard said, "I may have to move it to Reno." Jeffries replied: "I signed articles to fight in California. I do not want to go to Reno. Nothing in the agreement can make me change." Rickard then told him that if he didn't, it meant financial disaster and ruin. Jeffries wrote that he felt sorry for Rickard, that his good-nature got the better of him again. "All right, Tex, I'll go," Jeffries said, "but I am going so you will not lose your money. My better judgment tells me to stay away."[22] The training camp at Rowadennan was struck on June 21, and everyone traveled by automobile to Oakland to board the train for the "free and untrammeled state of Nevada."[23] A cartoon in the *San Francisco Examiner* pictured a grim-faced Jeffries balancing a trunk on his broad shoulders, a suitcase in his hand, walking across the California-Nevada state line, welcomed by an assortment of desert birds and beasts.

Governor Gillett's threat to bar all prize fights from California turned out to be an empty one. The *Reno Gazette* reported the following on June 24: "In spite of Governor Gillett's stand against prize fighting and his instructions to District Attorney Frederickson to stop tonight's fight, Abe Attell and Owl Moran fought their ten-round bout as scheduled."[24] The fight took place in Los Angeles and a decision was given. There were also two preliminary fights on the card. Other fights took place regularly in California, with only token opposition from reformers, and little or none by Governor Gillett and his Attorney General.

Jack Johnson did not appear upset when he heard the fight had been stopped. He told reporters he would meet Jeffries anywhere, and Nevada would be fine with him. In what was perhaps a parting gesture of defiance toward the California establishment, on June 21 Johnson opened up one of his fast cars on Ocean Boulevard between the Cliff House and Seal Rock House. He was pursued by patrolman Vincent H. Lewis, who followed Johnson into Seal Rock House, where Johnson locked the door of his private room against him. Patrolman Lewis went for assistance and returned with two more policemen. They broke down the door to Johnson's room and entered with drawn revolvers, where they found Johnson in bed leisurely reading a book. Told he was under arrest, Johnson left quietly with the police and walked to the front of the hotel, where a large crowd had gathered. Johnson offered to drive to police headquarters, and the four men, with Johnson driving his own car, took off for downtown San Francisco. On the way to the O'Farrell Street police station, Johnson gave his passengers a demonstration of what fast driving was all about. On the grade from First Avenue to Geary Street and Presidio Avenue, bystanders estimated that Johnson's car was traveling at least sixty miles an hour, the policemen in the back seat yelling for Johnson to slow down. When they arrived at headquarters, Johnson was taken before Police Chief John Martin, who said, "Hello, Jack. Arrested again?" "Yep," Johnson answered with his golden smile, "but it took three of them to bring me in." When Martin heard the complaint against Johnson, he told Johnson to post bail at the clerk's office. Bail was set at $10.00.[25] Johnson then left for Seal Rock House, where he gave an afternoon exhibition of boxing for reporters. He did not appear in court the next day. He forfeited the $10.00 bail and that was the end of the matter. He and his training companions left for Nevada on the evening of June 23.

"Nevada, The Last Free State"

Tex Rickard boarded the train at Oakland and left for Reno on Saturday evening, June 20. When the train stopped at Truckee, California, Rickard was surprised to see a delegation of old friends and partners from Goldfield, Nevada, who had waited for him there. Among this group were "Ole" Elliott and E. S. Highley, who told Rickard that Goldfield wanted the fight and was prepared to guarantee a sale of six thousand tickets at $20.00 each – or a total guarantee of $120,000. The offer was discussed in detail as the train wound its way down the Truckee River Canyon into Reno. As the train pulled into the Reno station, Rickard glanced out the window and saw a huge crowd gathered around the depot, waiting his arrival. When he appeared on the platform, he was given a rousing welcome by his fellow Nevadans and asked to say a few words. "You'll see the difference now," he said. "No more knocking [the fight] – only boosting, and everybody glad to see Nevada get the match. I was a fool ever to think of taking a big fight to the coast. Never again!"[1]

Rickard and his party made their way to Reno's Hotel Golden, usually headquarters for mining men in Nevada where the topic of conversation in the lobby was nearly always the latest mining strike. But now the conversation was about the fight, and the Golden was transformed into headquarters for the sporting crowd. As there were only fourteen days left before the scheduled fight, Rickard had to move swiftly. He had to get an arena built that would seat twenty thousand people. He wanted some assurance from Nevada Governor Denver Dickerson the fight would be allowed to go on without interference. And he had to select the site for the fight. Goldfield was bidding for it aggressively, and rumors circulated that their guarantee of $120,000 might be upped, if necessary to get it. The copper mining town of Ely in eastern Nevada was said to be interested. The relatively new and small mining camp of Mazuma in the Seven Troughs Mining District, with a population of only several hundred people, had put in a bid of $70,000. But no one took that bid seriously, as Mazuma had no railroad facilities and could be reached only by stage lines. Rickard told reporters he would meet with delegations from Reno and Goldfield late into the night and announce his decision the following day.

The next morning a rumor swept through the Hotel Golden that Goldfield had raised its offer to a $200,000 guarantee. That much money – and Goldfield had plenty of money – made people wonder if Reno was out of the running. Rickard went into a hurried conference with Elliott and Highley. They told him the offer was valid and if he needed further proof they would walk him over to the bank and show him a draft for that amount. Rickard was in conference most of the morning, talking with the Reno and Goldfield committees. Shortly after noon, Rickard announced his decision:

I have decided to hold the Jeffries-Johnson fight in Reno. In making the selection I wish to give my reasons for doing so. Goldfield made an offer which is hard to turn down. They are the *gamest lot of men I ever saw. This morning a committee of Goldfield businessmen offered to take me to a local bank and guarantee me a gate of $200,000. I decided on Reno, however, for several reasons. In the first place I did not feel that the fight fans of the east and west should be compelled to take that extra twelve hour ride across the hot desert to Goldfield. Then again the people from San Francisco can get here on the morning of July 4th and leave the same night in order to be back to their business Tuesday morning. For this reason I think probably one or two thousand more will come from San Francisco that would not go to Goldfield. The Reno people have done all they could. They will build a suitable arena and buy the $1,000 license for me.[2]*

As Rickard spoke, a brass band paraded down Reno's Virginia Street, passing the hat around, collecting money to build the arena. The entire amount needed to build the arena and to pay for the license was raised by private subscription.

Rickard had realized that Reno was the logical place for the fight because of its easy access by railroad. Reno had adequate switching facilities and yards to accommodate the heavy railroad traffic expected, and it was much closer to San Francisco than Goldfield. Had the fight been held in Goldfield it would have required another twelve hours of travel for sports coming from the north and another six hours for those coming from Los Angeles. While Goldfield had three railroads, it lacked adequate yards and switching facilities. As one member of the Goldfield committee said: "Distance and the long railroad haul beat us, but we were there with the coin." That afternoon Rickard drove around Reno looking for a site for the arena. The one he chose was the same used in 1905 when Marvin Hart had fought Jack Root, and where James Jeffries had acted as official referee. Jim McLaughlin, a local contractor, was hired to build the stadium, which to many seemed an impossible job to complete in thirteen days. But Nevada was a country where mining camps and boomtowns often blossomed overnight on the desert, and McLaughlin hired one hundred and seventy-five men to work ten hours a day on the structure.[3] Rickard opened a ticket office over the Palace Casino on Commercial Row and ordered tickets printed for the fight.

Rickard was aware the social reformers – flushed with victory in their efforts to stop the fight in California – had now focused their efforts on Nevada. He wanted some assurance from Governor Denver Dickerson that the State of Nevada would not intervene. For his part, Governor Dickerson, mindful of the rumors the fight was fixed, wanted assurances from Rickard that the fight was an honest one. Rickard gave the Governor his word the fight was not fixed, that it would be a fair fight. Then, on the evening of June 23, Governor Dickerson sent a telegram to Rickard and the *Nevada State Journal* in Reno. The *Journal* printed the text in a box on the front page:

> *By Governor D. S. Dickerson*
> *I believe the Jeffries-Johnson fight will be strictly on its merits, and so long as I am convinced as I am now of this fact, I will not interfere or make any effort to stop it. The laws of the state license this form of sport if the license is paid and the other requirements observed. If I was convinced that the fight was not to be on its merits, I would promptly see that it was not carried through in this state.*[4]

A few days later Governor Dickerson was again heard from when he unexpectedly walked into the lobby of the Hotel Golden and registered at the desk. A San Francisco reporter who was present described the Governor as a young man, smooth shaven, with brown eyes, wearing a tan summer suit and a large white Panama hat. He was recognized by other reporters and a score of Nevadans in the lobby, and a chorus went up, "Hello, there's the Governor." The eastern reporters were a bit skeptical that this was indeed the Governor of a state, expecting instead a portly man wearing a silk hat and frock coat, trailed by a retinue of lackeys, to say nothing of a marching band. The Governor smiled at the crowd and reporters asked, "How about the fight?" "I can say definitely," Dickerson replied, "there will be no interference from me. Any rumors that I have any intention of interfering in this matter are false. I wanted to be assured that this would be an honest contest. I have received that assurance, and I am satisfied. Under the laws of the state boxing contests are legal."[5]

Nevada was the only state where professional boxing was legal. Over the years it had played host to a number of important contests. The Bob Fitzsimmons-James J. Corbett championship fight had been held in Carson City, March 17, 1897, at the local race track. The Joe Gans-Oscar "Battling" Nelson fight in Goldfield on September 3, 1906, for the light heavyweight championship, attended by much national publicity, was Tex Rickard's effort to put Goldfield on the map, and his first fight promotion. Gate receipts totaled $70,000, setting a record. That fight lasted forty-two rounds and when it was over both fighters were exhausted. Joe Gans was a popular black boxer with Nevadans. When he was fouled by Nelson in the forty-second round the fans jeered Nelson, who lost the fight to Gans on a foul. Gans showed up again in Nevada in 1910 for the Johnson-Jeffries fight as a correspondent and wrote several syndicated feature articles about the fight. The fight at Tonopah between Joe Gans and "Kid" Herman on New Year's Day, 1907 did not attract as much attention as had the fight at Goldfield in 1906, but it was described in a memorable essay by novelist Rex Beach.[6] Beach, who had been a sourdough in the Yukon gold rush, gives us a vivid picture of Tonopah in 1907, descriptions of the fighters, and an account of the fight itself. The fight was filmed by motion picture cameras – an interesting fact in itself given the remote location of Tonopah at that time – and lighted by fifteen racks of mercury-filled tubes hung from the rafters above the ring, which colored everyone's face with a purple glow. Three moving picture cameras, each one loaded with a thousand feet of film, recorded the fight in a makeshift arena that had hurriedly been erected of raw lumber. In 1915, Jack Dempsey, who worked for a brief time as a miner in the Tonopah-Goldfield district, fought Joe Sudenberg first in Goldfield (which resulted in a draw) and a few weeks later in Tonopah. At that time Jack Dempsey was a green, inexperienced boxer, but he told his biographer, Nat Fleischer, that the Tonopah fight "was one of my hardest. I don't remember any other fight I ever engaged in which I was forced to extend myself more than in the picturesque Tonopah combat."[7]

Rex Beach suggested that professional boxing was legal in Nevada and nowhere else because Nevada represented the last vestige of a vanishing frontier, more rooted in the nineteenth-century than the twentieth.[8] The mining boom that swept across Nevada in the early part of the twentieth century certainly had all the ingredients of the frontier experience. Tonopah and Goldfield had blossomed in the Nevada desert almost overnight with the discovery of rich silver and gold deposits. This attracted the interest of thousands of boomtown adventurers, as well as money from the eastern capitalists. These people sometimes imagined opportunity where there was none, but they were willing to take risks, knowing that some had made millions. Tonopah and Goldfield provided the incentive and capital for mineral exploration throughout the state, and as prospectors made new strikes in remote locations, new mining camps were born: Manhattan, Rawhide, Round Mountain, Rhyolite, Wonder, Fairview, Seven Troughs, Rochester, National, Ely, Ruth, McGill, and others. There was a sense of opportunity and optimism in the air. As Rex Beach looked around the crowd in the

Tonopah fight arena he saw ladies in opera hats, furs, silks, feathered boas; others wore simple bonnets, cotton dresses, cloth coats. Some of the men sported patent leather shoes, white Stetson hats, fur-trimmed overcoats; others wore miners' boots, sheepskin jackets, denim, and leather caps. It was a motley assortment of people: some were working stiffs, others had struck it rich. There were even a few authentic prospectors and cowboys in the stands. The mere fact that so diverse a collection of people could come together in an arena built of rough lumber and rub shoulders demonstrated a kind of camaraderie and conviviality unique to the social history of mining camps. It was a scene that might have been played out in the Klondike a decade earlier, or in the Colorado gold camps in the 1880's. The rest of the nation, more conventional, or becoming so, looked upon Nevada with the forbearance and equanimity of a parent toward an unruly child.

*   *   *

In an effort to discredit the rumor that the fight was fixed, Ted Rickard issued a statement to the press that he hoped would settle the matter once and for all. He said the fight was absolutely on the square, that he had carried out the negotiations in a scrupulous and honest manner. Those who fostered the rumors of a "frame-up" were people who knew nothing of the fighters, he said, and their determination to win in a fair contest. He concluded saying: "We have tried out best to avoid any move in the staging of this contest that would lend the least semblance of truth to the vicious rumors and opinions that have gone the rounds."[9]

It was printed by most of the large newspapers across the country. On June 27, Rickard had to make another statement in response to a false report in a Chicago newspaper stating the fight had been called off. Rickard was concerned the rumor might discourage fans from making the trip to Reno. He said there was nothing to the rumor; he had it on good authority the rumor had been planted by a disgruntled reporter who earlier had been associated with rumors the fight was fixed.

With less than two weeks before the fight, the social reformers now launched an all-out effort to stop the fight. On June 20, George L. Rockwell, of Columbus, Ohio chairman of the "Stop That Fight" post card movement, which claimed a large share of success in stopping the fight in San Francisco, announced to the press that he would direct another movement of protest to Governor Denver Dickerson in Carson City. He stated ten thousand petitions directed to the Governor would be sent to prominent persons across the nation and petition circulators would be asked to get twenty thousand signers on each one. Attorneys for the "Stop That Fight League," he said, had advised him that there was no authorization in Nevada law for the fight as proposed. He contended the law on the books was passed only for the benefit of the Fitzsimmons-Corbett contest in 1897 and none other. Mandamus legal proceedings, he threatened, were underway to stop the fight. Mayor A. M. Britt of Reno was also the target of many letters of protest, though it was outside his jurisdiction, as the arena had been built outside the city limits of Reno. On June 21, the *Nevada State Journal* reported that all manner of influence was being brought to bear upon officials in Carson City to stop the fight. Governor Dickerson was in Oregon, but his secretary said it was impossible to reply to the thousands of cards and telegrams, that no response would be taken regarding them until the Governor returned. "Supreme court justices, the attorney-general of Nevada and prominent jurists have given their private opinions that there is nothing in Nevada law that would empower the Governor to interfere," the secretary said. "The law is plain and clear and makes this contest legal."

On June 25, the *New York Herald* carried a small story head-lined "Protests in Waste-Basket." It said that protests against the fight, both by mail and telegram, "continue to flood the office of Governor Dickerson, but they are promptly relegated to the waste basket, as the governor does not intend to interfere with the fight in any way."[11]

The city of Reno and its newspapers were caught up in the controversy when Rev. L. M. Burwell of the Methodist Church of Reno delivered a sermon to some four hundred people on June 26 condemning the fight. Denouncing the state law that permitted prize fights but admitting it was probably too late to stop the fight, Rev. Burwell titled his sermon "Reno's Disgrace." Reno was de-scribed as a "Godless wallower in the mire before the temple of Mammon," playing host to a horde of riffraff. "Reno is a city that de-lights in its saloons, gambling halls and divorce courts," Burwell said, "and the eagerness with which its citizens embraced the fight is the climax of mendacity." He added that Reno had sold all that is sacred and good for the sake of the dollar and in doing so had ex-posed its citizens and children to blight, and to a horde of crooks that would steal red hot stoves and ice out of refrigerators. He con-fided to his congregation that a Boston capitalist had told him on good authority the local politicians in Reno were all gamblers ex-cept for the mayor, who was a brewer of beer. "I am told ladies from the east intend to see the fight from a section of the arena screened off from the men so that they may be enabled to witness the exhi-bition without being observed by the male spectators," he said. "This is a crowning distinction between the people of the east and the west. The people of the east who come here know that what they do they should be ashamed to be caught at, but the people of the west are not even ashamed – they don't know what it is to be ashamed." Then Rev. Burwell turned his attention to Reno's news-papers. "The papers for weeks before the fight have devoted column after column to all the nauseating details of the work of the contestants and thus exalted as the supreme and most important thing of the day so base a spectacle and topic. To judge from the newspapers only seven persons in this city are opposed to the fight, and six of these are ministers. The newspapers have been urged on by the business men who are willing to have it appear the whole city is rotten." "Our work," Rev. Burwell concluded, "now has to do with the guilty, vice-polluted, stupefied Reno of today. You can't stop the fight now, I presume, but you can show the newspapers and the citizens you are opposed to it." In closing, Burwell called for a state law that would outlaw both prize fights and gambling.

In responding to Rev. Burwell, and in an ostentatious show of fair-mindedness (with perhaps a mischievous intent) the *Nevada State Journal* in Reno prominently featured the story at the top of the front page with a blazing two-column headline: "Unmerciful Roast Given Prize Fight Followers by Reno Methodist Minister," and with the sub-headline: "City Held Up as Wallowing in Mire with Off-scouring of the Country." The story is written with a liberal sprinkling of hyperbole, much of it quoted from the Rev. Burwell himself, and focuses upon what might be considered the more sensational remarks from his sermon, giving the reader the impression Rev. Burwell spoke with more bombast than reason. The style turns upon a kind of subtle *reductio ad absurdum*, and suggests such a diatribe might be expected of a soap box orator in a public park, but certainly not within the hallowed cloisters of the church.[12]

The social reformers had lost their campaign to stop the fight. Within a few days Reno would almost double in population as the crowds arrived for the great event. Some fans, knowing accommodations would be scarce to find, had come early. For the next ten days the nation's attention would be focused upon Reno.

"Reno, Center of the Universe"

When Jack London arrived in Reno, accompanied by "Boxcar Bill," his erstwhile traveling companion, he was among the first in a long list of celebrities who would walk through the gawking crowds gathered at the railroad depot on Commercial Street. It was as though the local grapevine had spread word of who might be arriving each day, and the crowds would turn out to catch a glimpse of some famous personality. It might be the grand old man himself, John L. Sullivan, or that legend of Dodge City, Bat Masterson, or former boxing champions "Gentleman" Jim Corbett, Bob Fitzsimmons, Tommy Burns, or perhaps Al Jolson, Rube Goldberg, Rex Beach, and of course the superstars of the moment, Jim Jeffries and Jack Johnson. A fanciful rumor made the rounds, probably inspired by some saloon wag, that Butch Cassidy himself had slipped into town incognito to see the fight.

When asked who his companion was, Jack London introduced him as "Boxcar Bill," a professional hobo who had come to Reno to see the fight. Bill had rode the rods as was his custom, while

London had occupied a comfortable Pullman. The party walked to a nearby saloon where London amused his audience. "Eighteen years ago I 'hoboed' it to Reno to attend Fair Week," he said. "I wanted to see the fair and I wanted to say I had been over the hill, so I set out for Reno from Sacramento. They rounded up a bunch of hobos when they got in on the freights and arrested them, but they never got me. I found the Sheriff's barn the safest place in town, and I slept there every night of Fair Week." London had praise for Reno and said that while eastern journalists might speak disparagingly of it, that was due to ignorance and sour grapes.[1]

London had a contract with the *New York Herald* to write a series of eleven articles about the fight. The *Herald* subsequently licensed the *Los Angeles Times* and the *San Francisco Chronicle* to publish his reports. In his first article, published June 24, 1910, London remarked there were more reporters in Reno to cover the fight than had been on the scene in Korea during the Russo-Japanese War. London knew what he was talking about, for he had been an overseas correspondent for the Hearst newspapers during that war. He had also been present at the Tommy Burns-Jack Johnson fight in Sydney, Australia in 1908 as correspondent for the *New York Herald* when Jack Johnson won the title from Burns. Nearly every large daily newspaper in the nation had at least one correspondent in Reno, and several national magazines were represented by famous writers of the day. While no one made a count of the number of journalists, there must have been several hundred. The volume of copy that would be sent out over the next twelve days would amount to millions of words. The *San Francisco Examiner* sent twelve reporters to Reno, which may have been the largest contingent. The Paris newspaper *Figaro* had sent M. Dupuy, and the *London Daily Mail* H. Hamilton Fyfe. Bat Masterson represented the *New York Telegram*, where he worked as a regular. Rex Beach, author of *The Spoilers* and other popular novels, had been contracted by the *Los Angeles Times* to write six articles for national syndication. These were published in the *Reno Evening Gazette* and newspapers across the nation. Beach wrote that while Robert Peary had fixed the axis of the planet at the North Pole, Tex Rickard had located the center of the universe in Reno, and that its magnetic attraction was drawing people from all over the world. With the fight still a week away, he wrote, there were more words going out over the wires from Reno than from Wall Street and Washington, D.C. The equivalent of two novels in newspaper copy were written every day and relayed to dozens of news syndicates. On the day of the fight, he predicted, bulletins would be flashed to every town in the land, crowds would gather in front of telegraph offices, and where matinee performances were held bulletins would be read to play-goers between the acts.[2]

Several articles by Jack Johnson and Jim Jeffries appeared in the press, though it is unlikely either man interrupted his training to sit down and put on a journalist's hat. They were probably written for syndication by ghost writers on the scene. John L. Sullivan was trying his hand as a special correspondent for the *New York Times*. Tom Sharkey contributed several pieces, as well as James Corbett, Sam Langford and Bob Fitzsimmons. As each day passed, the amount of space devoted to the fight in the pages of newspapers increased, until some of the sporting sections contained as much as ten to twelve pages, most illustrated with photographs. It is unlikely that any sporting event in the twentieth century commanded so much national attention in the press as the Johnson-Jeffries fight.

A crowd of five thousand had gathered at the depot on Commercial Street when Jeffries and his party arrived on June 27. So large a reception was usually accorded only to Presidents and reigning monarchs. But Jeffries did not like crowds and the hoopla associated with public curiosity. While the crowd waited, he slipped off the train at the far end and into his waiting automobile. He left it to James Corbett to take the bows and say a few words. The car sped away and headed for his training camp at Moana Springs, three miles south of downtown Reno. In the days to come the crowds would converge upon his camp, hoping to see him sparring with one of his partners, or punching the bags.

The crowd that waited for Jack Johnson's arrival the following day was not as large, perhaps because his train had been delayed three hours. The press reported Johnson was accompanied by his wife, but whether this was Belle Schreiber or Etta Duryea they did not say. In any case, Johnson was not married at this time, though common gossip had it he was. He made no effort to avoid the crowd as Jeffries had, nor did he play to the crowd. After waving his arms a few times, flashing his famous smile, he and his party made their way to two large touring cars and left for his camp at Rick's Resort, northwest of Reno.

To satisfy their editors, reporters had to turn out copy every single day, and one wonders what they found to write about in such voluminous detail. A good deal of it was speculation, of course, on the condition of the boxers and the outcome of the fight. But anything remotely associated with the event seemed newsworthy. Reports from the training camps made popular copy, written in a confidential tone so as to make the reader feel he was privy to some inside information. James Corbett, mouthpiece for the Jeffries camp, always made good copy. Tex Rickard was sought out for his opinions on everything from mining shares to the current betting odds. And when every subject seemed exhausted, journalists could always write something about Reno itself, the town that wore a cowboy hat, red suspenders, and a flashy kerchief. Eastern reporters were a bit puzzled by Reno. There was nothing quite like it anywhere else. One writer spoke of his traveling companion who, after a walk through town, returned to their Pullman car and said excitedly: "It's going on everywhere. Never saw anything like it."

"What?" asked the reporter. "Gambling. Wide open. Walk right in off the street. See a swinging door and push it open. Right inside you'll find roulette and faro and – and – I never was so tickled in my life! I lose twenty on faro before breakfast." Reno was a spicy little town built on the riot of chance, the writer said, with a district of saloons and casinos four or five blocks square. These establishments, with rough board floors and barren walls, operated some three hundred gambling games, running non-stop around the clock. Men of all types, he wrote, from the unwashed crapshooter from the Nevada mining camps to the sophisticated easterner, all laying down $10, $20, $50 bets while the roulette and craps bankers kept up a singsong and arcane chant. It was a snapshot, he wrote, of what Nevada stands for – a riot of gold, free and easy living, bankruptcy, flushness, despair, and delight.[3]

According to other journalists, Reno was infested with thieves, confidence men, and pickpockets who had come not to see the fight but to fleece the unwary. This was an exaggeration, of course, as was another reporter's statement that the city of Reno had only three policemen, two of whom were known to be derelicts. The usual contingent of ladies who had come to Reno for a quick divorce also made good copy, called "divorce-ease" by one writer. They could be spotted in Thomas' restaurant, gossiping over tea and cakes, or strolling around the courthouse lawn, passing the time away as they established a flash-in-the-pan residency to meet the requirements of Nevada's divorce laws. Such impressions never took note of the other Reno, the one of parks, public buildings, and fine homes. That there was another side to life in Reno either escaped the attention of these writers or was left out because such observations did not lend themselves to the kind of copy editors wanted. The tone of these articles is patronizing, written in a flip style, intended to amuse.

But the local press was not amused. Reno was being given a

bad press, and the local papers fought back. The *Reno Evening Gazette* ran a piece on the front page headlined: "Wild Stories About Reno Sent Out Far from Truth."

Some of the newspaper correspondents in Reno seem to have a desire to stray as far as possible from the truth in the stuff they are sending out; either that, or they have decided that it is easier to sit down and write what they think is going on, instead of exerting themselves to a little effort to find out the real conditions.

One well-known writer sent out under his signature a statement which would create the impression that the average price being charged for rooms in Reno is $10 a night. The Gazette has over 600 rooms listed, and the highest price asked for a large room, with double bed and use of bath is $2.50 a night. The average price being asked is $1.00 a night. The city is not yet overcrowded but one would gather from reading some of these wild stories that people are already sleeping in the park.

Reno has a right to expect better than this. It has been supposed that the newspapermen who are gathered here and who are coming are the pick of their respective staffs, men who realize that the accuracy is valuable in newspaper writing just as it is in other affairs. But apparently that is a supposition contrary to fact. Reno is doing its best to be hospitable to the visitors. Naturally, being a small city its resources will be taxed to the limit. But it is trying to give the stranger a fair deal, to keep prices down and to see that he is well taken care of. Consequently, stories similar to those cited are unjust.[4]

The *Nevada State Journal* also took up the defense, responding to the charge that "Reno and Nevada would stand for anything."

The Journal said Nevada had nothing to apologize for, that

*the charges were tainted with hypocrisy. "Nevada is on the level
with all and looks the rest of the world full in the eye, unabashed
and unashamed. It does not clothe its own unconventionalities in
euphemistic garb and apply harsh names to the unconventionalities of others. It has not outlived nor been schooled to abhor the
pioneer of western civilization, the gambler. It has not forgotten
that this entire territory was a gamble and a desperate chance that
broke right. It recognizes the propensity to gamble where everything is a gamble and has been from the beginning.*[5]

Some newspapers may have been chastised by this criticism.
The *San Francisco Chronicle* ran a story headlined: "Hungry
Sportsmen in No Danger of Famine." It went on to say that Reno's
restaurants were capable of feeding everyone, though there might
be delays. The story quoted W. O. Thomas, owner of Reno's largest
restaurant, who had made a survey of conditions, and who said his
restaurant had served two thousand meals on the previous day.[6]
Apart from the restaurants there were the saloons where, for the
price of a glass of beer, the visiting sport might partake of that
charming custom of the time, the free lunch. In most saloons at the
end of the bar there were assortments of breads, cold meats, pick-
led eggs, cheeses, and pickles, all for the taking.

Several days before the Fourth of July all hotel rooms in
Reno had been booked. For those who would arrive a few days before the fight, or the day before, a registry was set up at the Hotel
Golden to take care of those who had no reservations. The registry
listed rooms in private homes willing to take guests. In some cases
the Golden even provided porters to handle luggage and escort
guests to the private homes. In most Reno hotels cots were brought
out at night and placed in the lobbies and corridors where people
could sleep, for a nominal fee, of course. At the Golden when the
last dinner had been served shortly before midnight, the dining

room was converted into a dormitory filled with cots. Many sports who had traveled by train in Pullman cars made arrangements with the railroad to use the Pullmans for sleeping quarters. Switching engines moved the Pullmans to sidings in the railroad yard where they would be convenient to the sports yet not interfere with railroad traffic. If anyone slept in the parks it was by choice, not necessity. Even so, one San Francisco newspaper whose reporter must have known better could not resist drawing a sensational picture of an overcrowded Reno. "Reno is Sleeping in Parks and Cellars," the headline blared on page one. "Vast Crowds Line the River Bank, Many in Bath Rooms, Some in Chicken Coops. Bedless Try to Break into Churches. Many Walk the Streets All Night." To give the reader the impression the reporter had made a personal survey of conditions, the following statistics appeared in a box above the story: "Sleeping on the Slopes of the Truckee River, estimated 3,375. Fighting for Room to Sleep in the Public Parks, estimated 4,433. Sleeping on the Roofs of Houses, estimated 3,500. Sleeping in Funeral Parlors, estimated 135. Sleeping in the Morgue, Live Cases Only, 17. Sleeping in the County Jail, estimated all they can hold."[7]

The largest contingent of sports who would travel to Reno were expected to come from San Francisco and Oakland. Some five thousand were expected to make the trip, and the Southern Pacific Railroad, not having enough coaches and Pullman cars, ordered additional rolling stock (which included sixty Pullmans) from eastern railroads. The Southern Pacific had scheduled twelve special trains to Reno, each one bearing a name for the occasion: "Overland Limited," "Sagebrush Special," "Indoor Yacht Club Special," "Tom Corbett Special," etc. Tickets were priced at $11.15 for a round trip. Pullman accommodations were $1.50 extra each way, and the Pullman could be occupied during the stay in Reno. The "Sagebrush Special" was fitted out with coach cars and Pullmans, a dining car, a special barber, and waiters in Tuxedo jackets to serve refreshments. Specials were also scheduled to arrive in Reno from New York, Los Angeles, Portland and Seattle, Denver, Birmingham, Chicago, and St. Louis. So many passenger trains arrived in Reno the first days of July that freight traffic at division points across Nevada was either sidetracked or re-routed. A reporter asked the dispatcher at Reno how many specials might arrive on a particular day and he replied: "No one knows. They just come when they come. They are coming all the time but nobody seems to know how many there are. No more freight trains will be sent over this division until 6th of July."[8]

Others arrived by automobile caravan. One of the first to arrive was a group from Los Angeles, which came by way of Lake Tahoe. The women of the party were booked into a hotel at Glenbrook and left there to enjoy the pleasures of the lake and mountains while the men continued on to Reno. Other caravans wound their way to Reno from Seattle, Salt Lake City, Omaha, Denver, Boise, and Portland. The streets in Reno were crowded with automobiles of all descriptions: Packards, Stoddards-Daytons, Peerless, Nationals, Pope-Hartfords, etc. The local gasoline supply was almost exhausted when Southern Pacific announced that automobiles could fill their tanks at the railroad's shop yards in nearby Sparks.

Reno was becoming more crowded by the minute. The town was running wide-open around the clock. It was obvious an increased security and police force would be needed to handle the great influx of people, not to mention pickpockets and burglars, and possible acts of violence. "Anyone who thinks he will be able to secure an advantage by rough work will come to grief and will receive quarters at my boarding house," said Charles P. Ferrel, Sheriff of Washoe County. "There will be no intoxicating liquor sold, given away or disposed of in any way in the arena, and no matter what happens as a result of the fight, whether the public is satisfied or not, any attempt at disorder will be stopped instantly and effectively," he continued. The Sheriff announced that he had sworn in an extra forty deputies, many of whom would be positioned in the crowd in plain clothes, ready to respond should any trouble occur. "No one need be under any fear of uncertainty in coming to Reno," he added. "We will be in a position to handle a crowd of any proportion and by a system of divisions, squads, and a districting of the territory everyone will be as safe as in their own city."[9]

Acting upon a request from Sheriff Ferrel, Governor Dickerson announced on June 26 that the Nevada State Police, otherwise known as the Nevada Rangers, numbering some fifty men, would be sent to Reno under command of Captain Cox, "to see that the rights of the people are fully protected, not only on the day of the fight, but prior to the Fourth of July and for a couple of days after the Fourth." The *San Francisco Chronicle* reported: "Appointed by the Governor of the State, but working under civil rules, they are clothed with all the authority that the laws of Nevada will give them, and can go even further than the Sheriff or police in quelling any possible disturbances. Most of the State Police are mounted, and with their carbines, will be able to keep down any rioters who may appear on the scene. Captain Cox is already in Reno and will remain there until after the fight."[10] When former Governor Hutchinson of Idaho had his wallet lifted in the Palace Saloon, it was Captain Cox, in plain clothes and inconspicuous in the crowd, who chased the pickpocket down Commercial Row and caught the thief. The Governor's wallet was restored to him almost before he knew it had been pinched.

Jack Harrold, assistant chief detective for the Southern Pacific, after conferring with Sheriff Ferrel, announced the railroad would have forty detectives on duty to protect the traveling public, rolling stock, yards, and depot. One detective would be assigned to each Pullman car around the clock. Sheriff Ferrel and Mr. Harrold had exchanged "mug books" – containing photographs of known criminals – and promised that pickpockets and confidence men would be arrested as they stepped off the train. The railroad had stationed four detectives at Blue Canyon, California, to watch for hobos riding the rods to Reno, and one wonders how Boxcar Bill, who appeared with Jack London at the Reno depot, had managed to elude the railroad "bulls."

One reason for the elaborate security, at which Sheriff Ferrel had hinted, was to prevent any riot on the day of the fight should Jack Johnson win. If Jim Jeffries, the white hope, were to be defeated it was not unthinkable the crowd might turn ugly. Perhaps anticipating this, Tex Rickard had announced that no firearms would be permitted in the arena on the day of the fight. Detectives would be stationed at all gates to confiscate weapons and to search suspicious persons. Anyone found to be carrying a weapon who did not surrender it would not be allowed inside the arena, whether he had a ticket or not. Both Johnson and Jeffries (though each had his own bodyguards) would be escorted by police officers before and after the fight to prevent bodily harm to the two men. Considering the magnitude of the security problems, Sheriff Ferrel and his associates did a remarkable job, as did Captain Cox and the Nevada Rangers, and the railroad detectives.

MOANA SPRINGS
AND RICK'S RESORT

Shortly after their arrival in Reno, Jeffries and Johnson had resumed their training schedules. Jeffries had chosen Moana Springs as the site of his training camp, and Johnson had taken over Rick's Resort. Moana Springs was Reno's premier resort, certainly the more fashionable of the two. Whenever a rumor circulated that Jeffries was going to work out in the ring, the parking lot was crowded with automobiles, saddle horses, and bicycles lined up against the picket fence. At the entrance to the grounds was a large white building that housed the swimming pool and baths, fed by natural spring waters. There Jack London and Jeffries might sometimes be seen swimming, and London remarked the water was so sparkling and refreshing it made him feel ten years younger. Beyond the pool and baths were gardens and winding paths, flowerbeds, large shade trees, and ponds with ducks, geese, and rowboats. In this pastoral setting was a vendor's booth that sold cotton candy, and outdoor beer garden with stripped awnings, tables and chairs invitingly placed, and waiters to serve refreshments. Under a gazebo a young lady played a piano, singing a popular song of the day. Monkeys frolicked in the monkey cage. A small group of boys listened to "Gentleman" Jim Corbett tell how he had won the title from the great John L. Sullivan. Further on, in front of a white cottage, a crowd of onlookers strained their necks to catch a glimpse of the white hope himself, where he might be sitting on the porch, hidden by honeysuckle vines. In back of the cottage was the ring itself, about forty foot square, and to one side a small platform, with the punching bags. A crowd, seated on benches, waited for Jeffries to appear, and on the bag platform the cameras were set up.

They were often disappointed. Jeffries shunned publicity and the hoopla that went with it. When he was supposed to appear in the ring with a sparring partner, he went trout fishing instead. When he read in the newspapers accounts describing his physical condition as the marvel of the age, that once in the ring with Johnson he would prove invincible, he was disgusted. When he had signed the agreement to fight Johnson, he had no idea the publicity focused on the event would balloon to such enormous dimensions. Part of this was due, of course, to the "white hope" totem thrust upon him by the national press. By nature he was undemonstrative, often described as grouchy and taciturn. He would have made an excellent poker player, for men could look him full in the face and read nothing there at all. He seldom smiled.

On June 29, however, Jeffries did not disappoint his fans. Governor Dickerson had been invited by Corbett to watch Jeffries work out in the ring, and arrangements had been made with the motion picture people to shoot some footage of Jeffries in training. Word spread quickly through Reno and some two thousand people converged upon Moana Springs, so many that special trolleys were scheduled. The crowd surrounded the ring forty deep, some looked on from the roofs of buildings, or perched in trees. Others stood on picnic tables until several collapsed under the weight. Governor

Dickerson took the seat of honor, a rocking chair that had been placed at the edge of the ring. Promptly at four in the afternoon, Jeffries appeared in purple trunks, stepped into the ring, and a huge roar went up from the crowd. To start with, he skipped rope, some said he was nimble as a cat. An exhibition of bag punching followed, then some shadow boxing. Joe Choynski, a sparring partner, entered the ring and boxed two rounds with Jeffries, followed by Sam Berger, who sparred for two more rounds. The boxing, which many had looked forward to with such anticipation was a tame affair, nothing more than an exhibition for the motion picture cameras. Jeffries' partners were careful not to aim a blow at his head that might result in a cut, or strike a blow to the body that might bruise. With the fight only a few days off, Jeffries and his trainers wanted to be sure that he entered the ring against Johnson without any injuries, even minor ones. When the exhibition was over, Jeffries left the ring and disappeared into his cottage. Corbett came over to the Governor, spoke a few words and led him toward the white cottage, where Jeffries, after a hurried change of clothing, reappeared on the porch. The two men chatted and shook hands, posed for a few photographs, and the exhibition was over.

Earlier, on June 23, when John L. Sullivan had appeared at Moana Springs there had been another exhibition – but of a different kind. Sullivan had come in his capacity as a reporter for the *New York Times* and as the grand old man of boxing to pay a courtesy call on Jeffries and offer his best wishes. As it so happened, Corbett spotted Sullivan as he walked up the path to Jeffries' cottage. Corbett was in bad humor. He had been bothered with a back problem for several days, had not been sleeping well, a condition hardly calculated to improve his mood. Blocking Sullivan's path, he locked the gate to the cottage.

"What do you want?" Corbett asked.

"To see Jeff, of course," was Sullivan's answer.

"Mr. Jeffries," Corbett said stiffly, "does not wish to see you or have anything to do with you."

"Why is that?" Sullivan asked.

"We understand that you have been saying all over the country this fight is a frame-up in case Jeffries wins. You have never lost a chance to roast this fight and Jeffries has taken it much to heart."

"How do you know I have been knocking the fight?" Sullivan asked.

Corbett answered that it had appeared in the newspapers everywhere, and that on one occasion Sullivan had given a lecture at the Boston Athenaeum, where he was quoted by a reporter as having said so.

"I said nothing of the kind," Sullivan replied. "You have got it all wrong."

Corbett shot back, referring to their historic match in New Orleans in 1892: "I licked you in New Orleans and you never forgot that or forgave me. You have been knocking me all your life since then and the world over. When you came to me in New York and told me you were busted I said I would help you and in payment of that you have continued to knock me." Corbett went on to say that Sullivan, of all people, should be the last person in the world to knock the boxing game.[1]

Sullivan left, annoyed and humiliated, and took the trolley back to Reno.

At least two reporters were present during this exchange, and the story immediately went out over the wires, where it was picked up by nearly every newspaper in the country. One account said that Jeffries, sitting on the cottage porch with his wife, overheard the whole thing. Another had it Jeffries was not there, he was out doing roadwork.

There is nothing in the record to indicate Sullivan had ever knocked the fight, much less said it was fixed for Jeffries to win. An overzealous Boston reporter had concocted the story when he inferred Sullivan might be among those people who thought the fight was fixed. It had been written when editors wanted copy on the "fixed-fight" theory – but it was pure invention. Corbett could not have imagined the flap that ensued. It made him appear the villain of the piece, which he was in a sense, for he believed the rumors when he should have thought about them more critically. As former champion himself, he knew reporters sometimes misquoted or spun their stories to get a certain effect.

The next morning the newspapers were full of it. There was consternation in the Jeffries camp. Tex Rickard, who thought it was bad publicity for the fight, took it upon himself to issue a statement to the press:

Sullivan will be shown as much courtesy as any other newspaper correspondent. Sullivan's colleagues will be taken care of. John L. is the right man in the right place. There is no friction or trouble as far as I am concerned and Sullivan will never be barred from any arena of mine for expressing his opinion. If John L. is not at the ringside no one else will be there. I am with him heart and soul. TEX RICKARD.[2]

Behind the scenes, Rickard visited Jeffries' camp and did some hard talking. He must have been persuasive, for the next morning Jeffries sent an invitation to John L. at the Hotel Golden to visit his camp as his guest. Moreover, he issued a statement to reporters in which he apologized for Corbett's behavior, that had he been present when Sullivan was insulted, he would have taken "a good swift kick" to Corbett's backside. He said he was going trout fishing on the Truckee River on the morrow, and would be very pleased if Sullivan would join him.[3]

When Sullivan arrived the next morning it was a contrite James Corbett who met him at the cottage gate with a welcoming hand. They walked into the rubbing room where Jeffries got up from the table and greeted Sullivan. Corbett told Sullivan he regretted yesterday's incident and was ready to bury the hatchet. Sullivan was very gentlemanly, displaying the good humor and natural charm that had made him an icon with the public. Jeffries said: "It is all right now and we should be good friends. I am willing it should be so between us all."[4]

In his column dated June 24, 1910, John L. gave a straightforward version of the event. His version of the verbal exchange with Corbett was not so detailed as other accounts, but the gist of it was clear enough. He referred to the old rivalry between himself and Corbett, had not seen Corbett for years, and was surprised when an unforgiving Corbett challenged his appearance at the gate to the cottage. For himself, Sullivan said considering the troubles the contest had gone through, his only concern was to help it along in every way possible. How foolish it would be, he wrote, for him, once a champion, to decry the sport that had made him famous, and the sport he loved.[5] To everyone's credit, the flap was soon forgotten. The story vanished from the newspapers almost as quickly as it had appeared.

The question of the hour was whether Jeffries had reached the peak of his physical conditioning. Jeffries said he had. In an article that carried his byline, he wrote: "The way I feel now in my present shape I do not think there's a man in the world who would have a chance to lick me. I do not say this to be boasting, but I want to be on the level and let my friends all over the country know what I think of my chances."[6] He explained to a disappointed public he had not boxed more because he did not want to take the edge off his training, that he was at the top of his form, and no one could be a better judge of condition than himself.

Jeffries might have boxed more had it not been for the crowds at Moana Springs, preferring the privacy and isolation of the camp at Rowadennan. He felt no obligation to entertain people who had no claim on him, and he did not want sparring sessions to become simple entertainments. To escape the throngs that daily took trolleys out to Moana Springs, he did his exercise routines and roadwork early in the morning, and then left to go trout fishing on the Truckee River. Evenings he played hearts or gin rummy with his close friends at a picnic table on the lawn of his cottage. While he played cards, Corbett kept unwanted visitors away. Mrs. Jeffries looked on, busy with her knitting in a lounge chair under a cotton-wood tree.

But beneath this tranquil scene Jeffries felt the tension of the upcoming fight. There was a hint of it in his column when he wrote: "For more than one year I have been keeping faith with the public, which demanded this match."[7] To those who knew him intimately it was clear he did not enjoy his role as the "white hope." The only relief he could find was in trout fishing, in a setting where he could be alone with his thoughts, away from the crowds. The press, how-ever, portrayed him in the days before the fight as a man supremely confident, without a worry in the world. The last day before the fight he went fishing in the morning, played hearts in the afternoon, and went for an automobile ride. After dinner he walked across the road to a gambling casino where he played dice for ten minutes with a stake of twenty five dollars. He lost.

*   *   *

Rick's Resort lacked most of the attractions of Moana Springs. It had no swimming pool, no beer garden or shady paths that wandered through a garden setting. Located three miles south-west of downtown Reno, it could not be reached by trolley. But it was a fairly new resort, an attractive house of three floors, with an expansive porch on three sides decorated with white columns. Young trees had been planted at the entrance but they were not yet large enough to provide much shade. The interior was spacious enough, the floors were polished, and curtains made of champagne corks separated the rooms on the ground floor. In the room nearest the entrance was the casino, which offered a roulette wheel and dice table. Beyond was a dance floor with a piano. A bar separated the dining room and the dance floor. The rooms on the second floor, complete with baths, had all been booked by Johnson and his party. In back of the main house a platform had been built of hardwood, covered with mats and enclosed with ropes. This was the ring in which Johnson sparred with his partners. To one side was a bag platform. In the rear were a few small cottages.

If Jeffries' camp was off-limits to the general public, Johnson's was just the opposite. It seemed everyone was welcome. Sports writers could always count on Johnson to say a few words for publication. Spectators who drove out the Laughton Road to Rick's could watch the champion box with a sparring partner, work out on the bag platform, throw the medicine ball, and perhaps even exchange a few words with Johnson. He made the grinding ordeal of training look easy. He always seemed in good humor, even after ten miles of road work, cracking jokes with his companions to get the lead out of their shoes and keep up with him. Whatever he did he kept up a constant chatter – trading quips with a sparring partner, or tossing remarks at spectators at ringside. Sometimes he would clown around before an impromptu audience, demonstrating a slow-motion punch that would demolish Jeffries' famous protective crouch. One time he chased a flock of chickens for reporters, caught one, held it up flapping, and said he had learned the trick of catching them in his youth. After a rubdown one evening, reporters watched him shoot dice with some of his companions, and said that Johnson was pretty good at rolling the bones. Or he might give them a bit from his vaudeville act, drag out the bull fiddle and play a tune. A few reporters took all this to mean Johnson wasn't very serious about his training, described him as simple and frivolous. But they missed the point. Johnson worked hard and trained every day, and he was deadly serious about it.

While Jim Jeffries sat grim-faced under the shade trees at Moana Springs and spurned the adulation of fans, Johnson welcomed them. The trouble was there weren't many of them. When people had shouted good wishes to Jeffries he had grunted in reply – if he responded at all. Johnson grinned from ear to ear, flashing his famous smile. There were few black people in Reno for the fight; the trip was too expensive for most. But Johnson had his day on June 28. Governor Dickerson had announced he would visit Johnson's camp that day and watch Johnson work out with his sparring partners. Some three hundred people either walked or drove out to Rick's, and Laughton Road was crowded with pedestrians, automobiles, bicycles, and saddle horses. The motion picture people were there. John L. Sullivan was there, and while the crowd waited for Johnson to appear, John L. entertained the crowd by punching the bags. Stanley Ketchel was there, who took his turn punching the bags, then posed for a photograph with John L. Johnson had done ten miles of roadwork that morning, and after a rubdown he took a short nap. When he woke he heard the crowd outside and changed into his boxing trunks and robe. Passing through the casino downstairs, the clink and whir of the roulette wheel caught his fancy. He stopped and asked for twenty dollars in chips, made bets on 32, 33, 34, 35, and 36, his favorite roulette numbers. None of them came up. He asked for another twenty dollars in chips and hit 35.[8] Satisfied, he walked outside and climbed into the ring. He spotted Tex Rickard sitting on the grass with Governor Dickerson and Captain Cox of the Nevada Rangers, smiled at them and began punching the bag on the bag platform. He circled the bag several times, hitting it from various angles, increasing his rhythm, when the frame supporting the bag started to vibrate and suddenly the bag flew out into the audience. It struck Ben Benjamin, a sports writer for the *San Francisco Chronicle*, breaking his glasses and causing a cut over one eye. Benjamin was quickly revived and taken by automobile to Reno for treatment.[9]

Al Kaufman, one of Johnson's sparring partners, entered the ring. The two men squared off and boxed for two rounds. Though Kaufman boxed cautiously and several times penetrated Johnson's guard, he received several whipping jabs from Johnson, who seemed to place his punches exactly where he aimed them. Johnson gave everyone the opportunity to see his neat blocking and fast defensive work. At the end of the second round Johnson let fly a series of jabs and hooks that brought applause. Then came George Cotton, veteran sparring partner and an excellent boxer in his own right, for an exhibition of four rounds. Cotton came on strong and fast, but Johnson picked off the blows and kept Cotton off balance with counter-punches and some dazzling footwork. The crowd sensed they were watching a real boxing exhibition, one that displayed everything that could happen in a fight. They were right. In the fourth round Cotton came in like a whirlwind, found an opening in Johnson's defense, and shot a left to Johnson's mouth. A stream of blood trickled down the champion's chin. Johnson countered with two blows to Cotton's face which snapped his head back. But Cotton continued to bore in, slugging with both hands. They clinched, and Johnson worked his left arm free and landed a hard left hook full on Cotton's jaw. Cotton's legs folded and he fell to his knees, his body falling unconscious over the ropes. It was a knockout. Everyone was impressed. Governor Dickerson turned to Tex Rickard and asked, "Is that boy hurt?" Then: "Suppose Johnson had been knocked out, would it have spoiled the Johnson-Jeffries fight?"

Rickard replied Cotton was all right, that it was unlikely Johnson would have been knocked out in his own training quarters. Then Rickard asked the Governor: "Have you ever seen any fights where men have been knocked out?" "Well, yes," Dickerson replied. "I have seen men knocked out in fights but not with gloves. Gloves were not the weapons in those fights."[10]

When asked for an opinion of the exhibition, John L. Sullivan said: "These fellows [Johnson's sparring partners] are playthings for him, and the work today is no criterion of what may be expected in the ring. Johnson seems in fairly good trim, however, and he is certainly working happily and without any forcing."[11] Sullivan may have hedged his remarks, remembering Corbett's accusations, because he did not wish to appear to favor either fighter. Sullivan had met the black champion earlier, when Johnson was in California at his training camp at Seal Rock House. There is a famous photograph of the two men shaking hands, Johnson dressed in a hat and overcoat, with Billy Delaney standing between the two men. Some boxing historians have assumed this picture was taken in Reno, apparently without wondering why anyone would be wearing an overcoat in Reno in June or July, where temperatures reached into the mid-nineties each day. If further proof were needed that this photograph was not taken in Reno, it was published in the *San Francisco Examiner* on Wednesday, June 22, 1910, opposite a column written by John L. before Johnson moved his training camp to Reno. The photograph also appeared on a post card, without any caption, and was probably taken by Percy Dana, San Francisco sports photographer. Temperatures in San Francisco – especially at Seal Rock – can be quite chilly in June and July, which explains the overcoat Johnson wore.

Percy Dana was in Reno several days before the fight and acted as official photographer for the *Reno Gazette*. His studio was in San Francisco at 1345 Fillmore Street but he traveled often to photograph boxing events in California. The *Reno Gazette* said of him: "Photographer Dana of San Francisco as genial and accommodating a man as he is a clever picture taker, is doing some fine work and quick work here. He's the busiest man in town among the fight people. Most of the illustrations of the *Gazette* are but examples of his expert work." [12] Dana took hundreds of photographs before and during the fight, including a set of one hundred and twenty real photo post cards, most centering on the fight itself. With the discovery in the 1980s of some twelve hundred of his original glass plate negatives in San Francisco,[13] Dana has come to be regarded as the photographer *par excellence* of American boxing. The collection includes glass plates in various sizes, most in fine condition. His work includes pictures of James Corbett, Stanley Ketchel, Battling Nelson, the original Joe Walcott, Joe Gans, Jack Johnson, James Jeffries, Sam Langford, Jimmy Britt, Tommy Ryan, Hugo Kelly, Billy Papke, Antone LaGrave, and a host of others. The collection includes actual fight photographs in the ring as well as portraits taken in his studio. Dana was an accomplished photographer, and his dedication to the sport of boxing provides an invaluable photographic record to anyone interested in its history. Another still photographer who was on the scene was William E. Cann, who owned a drug store on Reno's Commercial Row. Cann took photographs for post cards which he sold in his store. He also sold a line of photographic equipment and souvenirs of the Johnson-Jeffries fight, such as posters, books, and color photos of Johnson and Jeffries in a tube ready for mailing at five cents each.

The motion picture people were pleased with the roughhouse style of the boxing exhibition, especially the knockout of George Cotton. Motion pictures were still relatively new to the American scene, and people all over the country flocked to theaters to watch films of Johnson and Jeffries in training. The Vitagraph Company of America, owned by William T. Rock, had signed with

Rickard, Johnson, and Jeffries for exclusive rights to the fight, and for sequences to be filmed at the training quarters. Potentially, the fight film promised more money in returns than either the purse or the gate receipts. Rock estimated it would cost $25,000 to film the fight. There would be three separate cameras at ringside, each with a crew of several men. Each camera would be filming simultaneously, so the company would have three separate negatives of the fight, each from a different camera angle. Rock also had chartered a special train to rush the film to New York for processing. He expected within one week some five hundred prints of the film would be distributed to theaters across the land.

Rock was so convinced the film would prove to be a gold mine that he approached Johnson with an offer to buy out his interest. He offered Johnson $50,000 for his share, and Johnson accepted. He next approached Rickard and Jeffries, and offered $50,000 to Jeffries and $25,000 to Rickard. Both men accepted the offer.[14] As matters turned out, it proved to be a disaster for Rock, but a prescient and profitable move for Johnson, Jeffries, and Rickard. The only condition Rock had stipulated was that the fighters enter the ring and begin the fight. What Rock did not foresee was that the fight film would provoke a firestorm of controversy, that it would be banned in most American cities (at the urging of social reformers and politicians), and that it would subsequently be banned in Europe, Australia, New Zealand, and Canada. Rock's dream of a windfall was turned into a nightmare.

An interesting sidelight to the deal Jeffries signed with the Vitagraph Company – in which he sold his share of the film rights for $50,000 – involved Mrs. Jeffries and a dispute over attorney's fees. Jeffries had asked a local Reno attorney to draw up the contract for the sale of the motion picture rights. The attorney prepared the contract, which was presumably signed with Mr. Rock. A day or so later, the bill for drawing up the contract arrived at Moana

Springs, charging a fee of five thousand dollars. When Mrs. Jeffries saw the bill she hit the roof, described it as exorbitant and outrageous. While Jim Jeffries sat under the shade trees at his cottage and played hearts, Mrs. Jeffries took the trolley downtown to Reno and confronted the attorney in his office. After giving him a piece of her mind, she said the bill would not be paid, and tossed it on his desk with a flick of her wrist. Mrs. Jeffries was usually a quiet and retiring woman, but on this occasion her temper flared, and the flustered attorney, not wanting to become embroiled in a public colloquy, backed down. A revised bill, reduced by half, arrived in the mail the next day and was paid by Jeffries' manager.[15]

To the casual observer the mood at the Johnson camp appeared to be jovial and easygoing. But trouble had been brewing between Johnson and his business manager, George Little, for some time. It came to a head in San Francisco, at the Seal Rock House, on June 11 when Johnson attempted to get a warrant for the arrest of Little on the charge that Little had stopped payment of a check that Johnson had cashed for him. Johnson stated he had cashed a check for $300 drawn by Little on the night of June 3, that he placed the check in a San Francisco bank for collection and that the Chicago bank on which the check was drawn returned it, saying that payment on it had been stopped by Little. In his defense, Little had replied that he had not stopped payment on the check until Johnson had fired him as manager. Little, who had negotiated the contract with Tex Rickard for the Johnson-Jeffries fight, was outraged. "I have a contract," Little said, "he can't do this to me."[16] But Johnson did, though it cost him $26,500, which he paid out of the sale of his share in the motion picture rights. Little was replaced by Sig Hart. Johnson said he had fired Little because of a bitter dispute that occurred during a poker game, adding that Little had grown so zealous of his position as business manager that he resented other members of the Johnson camp. But the real reason for the breach between the two men may have run deeper. In newspaper accounts describing Johnson's settlement with Little, a diamond brooch belonging to Little is mentioned, valued at $2,000.[17] This was returned to Little as part of the settlement when Johnson bought out his contract.[18] According to one of Johnson's biographers,[19] Little had begun to take an interest in Etta Duryea (who was not married to Johnson at the time), and gave her the diamond piece as a token of his affection. Little may have noticed that Etta was unhappy with Johnson, who continued to show an interest in, if not attraction to, Belle Schreiber. If so, he may have regarded it as an opportunity to make his move. In any case, Johnson somehow found the diamond brooch, and the cat was out of the bag.

Without a fighter to manage, George Little went to Reno, where he hoped to arrange a match between the winner of the Johnson-Jeffries fight with Sam Langford. But nothing came of it. Johnson remarked he had heard rumors in Reno that Little was talking against him, betting heavily on Jeffries to win.[20] But in remarks to the press, Little stated that he and Johnson were on friendly terms, that he was betting on Johnson to win, and that Jeffries would not lay a glove on Johnson inside the first ten rounds.[21] Little may have been trying to put the best face upon a relationship that had gone sour, so much so that he was declared *persona non grata* at Johnson's training camp.

Etta had been at Johnson's training camp at Seal Rock in California when Johnson broke with Little. She had kept in the background, to herself. When the fight was cancelled in California, she was probably more annoyed about the change in arrangements than was Johnson. But she did follow him on the train to Reno, though where she stayed while in Reno is anyone's guess. She was not present at Rick's on June 28 when Johnson gave the boxing exhibition for Governor Dickerson and the motion picture people, at least there is no mention of her in newspaper accounts. Perhaps be-

cause of tension between her and Johnson over the George Little affair, or perhaps because she felt out of place in the excitement generated by the upcoming fight, she unexpectedly returned to San
Francisco. Johnson, who may have acted on impulse, promptly sent
a wire to Belle Schreiber in Chicago and asked her to come to Reno.
Belle was delighted, guessing that Etta had left Johnson and the
field was again open. A curious story appeared in the *Los Angeles
Times*[22] about a mysterious young blond woman who boarded the
Overland Limited in Chicago on June 27. She was described by passenger as well-dressed in a tailored costume, possessed of an exceed-
ingly good figure, and so stunning in appearance she attracted
everyone's attention in the Pullman. However, she kept to herself
and would not be drawn into conversation. On the second day of
the trip two women sitting within earshot of the mysterious blond
began a conversation about the upcoming fight, which was a natural topic of conversation as the train was carrying three coaches of
fight fans to Reno. The two women talked of Johnson and his white
"wife," and one expressed her opinion about Johnson's "wife" in
very uncomplimentary terms. The blond woman, who must have
overheard everything, expressed no emotion or interest whatever.
When it was learned from one of the porters that the blonde's des-
tination was Reno, speculation circulated in the Pullman that she
might be a famous actress, or possibly the wife of an industrialist or
banker bound for Reno to get a divorce. As the train approached
Reno, the blond prepared to leave the train. Her fellow passengers
were either in the Pullman or gazing out the dining car window
when they saw the red brick depot in Reno pull into view. Waiting
at the side of the depot was a large black touring car, and beside the
car stood Jack Johnson himself. The blond stepped from the train
and was immediately swept into an embrace by Johnson, who led
her to his car. The secret was solved. The blond woman was Jack
Johnson's "wife," the story said, and the garrulous lady of the day

before who had expressed her opinion so loudly fainted in her seat, and could not be revived until the train had left Reno. The story probably contains some hyperbole, if not errors in fact. The young blond woman, who was not identified by name, was Belle Schreiber, responding to Johnson's wire.

When Etta heard Belle had arrived in Reno she was furious. She took the train back, confronted Johnson and read him the riot act. She may have offered him a choice: either Belle went, or she went. What precisely happened is not known. In any case, Belle conveniently disappeared. Etta remained in Reno. Photographs taken at the time of Etta and Belle – and they are few – are captioned "Johnson's wife." No further identification is given. One photograph of Johnson's "wife" shows an unsmiling woman with a somewhat blank expression seated in the back of a large touring car. This is unmistakably Etta. Another photograph, taken by William E. Cann of Reno, shows a vivacious and smiling young woman – unquestionably Belle Schreiber – seated between Johnson's legs, his arms around her waist. They are flanked on either side by members of Johnson's staff, seated on porch steps. This photograph was most likely taken at Rick's Resort and bears the caption: "Johnson and Wife, Reno, Nev." Then there are two photographic post cards by Dana that show Johnson's "wife" present at the fight. One has a notation that reads: "Johnson's wife at ringside." The other card is captioned in the negative: "No. 41. Mrs. Johnson Cheering the Champion." The woman in both these photographs looks very much like Belle Schreiber, and seems to contradict the story that Johnson sent Belle packing back to Chicago. It would have been typical of Johnson to tell Etta he had sent Belle away while he had in fact secreted her in a hotel somewhere in Reno. If this is so – and the photographs seem proof – then Johnson was not being honest with Etta. The evidence suggests that Belle may have attended the fight and Etta did not. In Johnson's autiobiography[23] there is a picture captioned "My Party at the Jeffries Fight," which shows Johnson, two women, and two men. This picture was not taken at Reno, and neither of the two women are Etta or Belle. It may have been taken on one of Johnson's many vaudeville tours, possibly in Europe. Johnson is wearing a heavy fur coat, both women are wearing furs (one with a fur muff), and the men are wearing overcoats, hardly appropriate for Reno in the month of July. If this is not confusing enough, Johnson further confused matters when, in Reno, he introduced on separate occasions both Etta and Belle to people as "my wife." There is even the possibility that he introduced both women as "my wife" to the same persons (not on the same occasion, however) making people wonder how many "wives" he actually had. But then Johnson may have wanted people to be confused, not only about his women, but other things as well. It probably amused him to keep people guessing. He knew the betting odds were running against him – people were betting on Jeffries to win – and this probably amused him too.

THE FIGHT OF THE CENTURY

The morning of the Fourth of July dawned bright and sunny over Reno. The air was fresh and crystal clear. It was the big day. People were up early, eager to hear the latest news from the training camps, and the latest picks of the experts. Stanley Ketchel, who at the time was the world's middleweight champion, picked Johnson to win. He had talked with Johnson on the veranda at Rick's the previous afternoon and said that Johnson was completely relaxed, preferred listening to music rather than talk about the fight. Ketchel said the first three rounds would give an indication of how the fight would go. Johnson's chances, he said, would be better in a long fight. Approximately three months later, on October 15, 1910, Stanley Ketchel would be murdered, shot in the back by a jealous rival in a romantic triangle. The shooting occurred on a ranch near Conway, Missouri, where Ketchel had gone to enjoy a period of extended rest. Joe Choynski, now a sparring partner for Jeffries, was the Polish-Jewish heavyweight whom Johnson had fought in Galveston, Texas in 1901 (after which both fighters had been thrown into jail) picked Jeffries to win in seven rounds. He believed Johnson's only hope was to put up a brilliant defense and perhaps wear Jeffries down. But given Jeffries' enormous strength, he said, this was not likely. If Johnson tried to trade blow-for-blow with Jeffries, he would not last seven rounds, he said. Tommy Burns, still rankled over losing the title to Johnson in Australia in 1908, said with poor grace: "I learned that the big Negro is not much of a fighter, though he's a good boxer. Johnson's left hand is of little use to him. He can't use it as freely as his right – certainly there is no knockout in it."[1] John L. Sullivan, after "studying the dope" – as he put it – picked Johnson to win. George Cotton, Johnson's chief sparring partner, said: "Johnson is the greatest boxer that ever pulled on a glove. It is next to impossible to hit him. I know that he can hit. I know that he has the heart and confidence. He will surprise some wise bettors. I know Jack will win decisively, but it will be a hard fight."[2] Walter Monahan, a classy light heavyweight said: "You have seen me box with Johnson. I am lighter and faster on my feet than he, but I could not begin to get away from him. Jeff is going to be duck soup for Jack. He will hit him at will and get away from counters. You can put me down for any round between the tenth and twentieth."[3] James Corbett, solidly in Jeffries camp, picked Jeffries to win in ten rounds. George Little, despite his differences with Johnson, picked Johnson to win. Battling Nelson, former lightweight champion, said: "Johnson will win, because he is in better condition than Jeffries, because of his youth and because no fighter was ever able, after leaving the ring for any length of time, to 'come back.'"[4] Tom Jones, a fight manager who would later manage Jess Willard, picked Jeffries, saying that Johnson was yellow and had no stomach for a pitched fight.

Johnson released a statement to the press saying he felt confident he would win. "I do not say this with any intent to infer that I do not consider Mr. Jeffries a dangerous opponent. A man of his bulk and strength is a hard man to handle at any time, and I know that Jeffries is a good boxer and a hard hitter, but I feel confident that I can show as much and more in all of these lines. Although I am satisfied that I will be the winner, I still have enough sporting blood in my veins to say: 'May the best man win.' "[5] Jeffries said of himself: "I am sure that I will be able to go strong whether the fight is long or short. It makes no difference to me. I have worked hard and long for this occasion and I am going to make the best of it. I want it understood that if Johnson should lick me I will have no excuse to offer. Win or lose, I will retire. This is my last fight and I am going to make it a winning one."[6]

Odds on the fight were determined by the betting parlors in Reno and San Francisco. Jeffries was an early favorite from the moment the betting started. In the early betting, which was unusually light, Jeffries was favored to win by 10 to 6. These odds fluctuated from day to day, and on the morning of the fight the odds stood at 10 to 7 in favor of Jeffries. There was a great deal of money bet on Jeffries, some of it in large chunks, while the money on Johnson came in smaller bets. To cover a $5,000 bet on Jeffries it was necessary to find several smaller bets on Johnson to cover the $5,000. In Wall Street, the betting was unusually light, with less than $10,000 down on July 2. The largest single bet recorded on the street was one of $2,500 on Jeffries to $1,400 on Johnson, booked by members of the exchange. On the Consolidated Exchange, several wagers of $1,000 to $600 were recorded. One bet of $500 was made at even odds that Johnson would win in ten rounds. One broker reported an unnamed client had deposited $10,000 with him to bet against $100,000 that Jeffries would win in the seventh round.

In Reno the betting parlor over the Palace Casino posted the odds on betting by rounds. One to five rounds: Jeffries 34, Johnson 3. Six to nine rounds: Jeffries 30, Johnson 5. Ten to fifteen rounds: Jeffries 30, Johnson 6. Fourteen to eighteen rounds: Jeffries 34,

Johnson 17. Nineteen to twenty-four rounds: Jeffries 36, Johnson 32. Twenty-five rounds and over: Jeffries 46, Johnson 32. These odds indicate that Johnson's chances of winning improved after the thirteenth round, should the fight last that long.

Johnson was so confident of winning that he bet $5,000 on himself with Jimmy Lawlor, who ran a betting parlor across the street from the Palace. And later, when Hector McKenzie, an eastern bookmaker visited the Johnson camp, Johnson took him to one side and said: "I hear you have some money to bet against me and I think I would like to win your money."[7] As it turned out, Johnson bet $1,000, his training staff chipped in $500 more, and McKenzie laid down $2,500 against their $1,500. When the big bettors – or high rollers as they are called today – began placing their bets, it made news. James A. Murray, who owned banks in the Pacific Northwest, rolled into Reno in his private railroad car and announced he had $5,000 to bet on Johnson to win. This bet was immediately covered by George Consodine and Nat Goodwin, the latter a Nevada theatrical producer and confidence man. E. M. Smathers of New York City, a flamboyant turfman who had recently won $$50,000 by betting on the winning horse in the Twentieth Century Handicap at Chicago, announced he had $10,000 or $15,000 to bet on Johnson. This bet was covered by copper tycoon Robert F. Guggenheim. James Corbett, Jeffries' most vocal supporter, bet $5,000 on Jeffries to win. Ed McKeown, a turfman from Winnipeg, Canada arrived with $10,000 to bet on Johnson. Most of the big money, however, was bet on Jeffries, at odds of 10 to 7 in favor of Jeffries.[8]

At the arena, workers busied themselves putting numbers on seats and boxes so that ushers could show ticketholders to their respective seats. The arena had been built to seat 16,000 people, not large enough to accommodate everyone who had come to Reno to see the fight. An additional 3,000 standing-room-only tickets were issued and sold at the gate just before the fight. These standees were packed like sardines into the extreme outer circle of the arena. Scalpers were busy at the entrances hawking tickets they had bought earlier, doubling or tripling the price. Gate receipts exceeded Tex Rickard's expectations. Slightly over $300,000 in tickets were sold. This was the largest gate ever for a boxing match anywhere in the world.

Private boxes for ladies attending the fight were located at the top of the funnel-shaped arena, fitted out with curtains against prying eyes and the curious. When asked if she planned to attend the fight, Mrs. Jeffries said absolutely not, she would remain at Moana Springs and get the results by telephone. Etta Duryea was in seclusion, not available for comment, but when reporters asked Johnson if "his wife" would be there he said yes, she would. John L. Sullivan said she was there, in the sixth row on the right side of the arena, and at the end of the tenth round she stood up and shouted, "Keep it up, Jack." But this does not sound like Etta, given her state of mind at the time. More than likely it was Belle Schreiber. However, a number of ladies did attend, setting a new fashion for the sport of boxing. Mrs. Tex Rickard hosted a party of ladies in her private box, including Mrs. Rex Beach, Mrs. Harry Eppinger of San Francisco, Mrs. James Corbett, Mrs. James Kelley of Los Angeles, Mrs. Jack Kepper, wife of Jeffries' Los Angeles partner, Mrs. Jack Jeffries, Mrs. Otto Floto, wife of the circus owner, and others. It has been estimated that one hundred ladies attended the fight.[9] The *Nevada State Journal* published an account of the fight by a woman – certainly a novelty for the times – whose byline simply read "By I. M. W." In her opening remarks this lady chastised the "moralists" who criticized the fight and the easterners who heaped scorn and insult upon Nevada and Nevadans, and said such people who were sure they knew what they were talking about and believed what they wanted to believe had nothing to reveal but their own ignorance.[10]

Crowds from downtown began moving out to the arena as early as eleven in the morning, though the gates would not open till noon. The two cars of the Reno Street Railway were so jammed to capacity that most people walked to the arena – a distance of one mile – just outside the city limits. By noon thousands were lined up at the four entrances. When the gates opened, the crowds filed through turnstiles in an orderly manner and poured into the arena. In less than fifteen minutes the gallery seats and the wide platform encircling the outer-rim were half-filled. The cool morning breeze could not enter the arena because of its construction – in the shape of a funnel – where the heat from the sun was trapped and the raw wooden boards seemed to absorb the sun's rays. Many sports put on smoked glasses and green eye-shades and shed their coats and collars. Shortly before one o'clock the Reno Military Band played several selections, including "America," "The Red, White and Blue," "Dixie," and others. Some writers have written that the band played a tune deliberately insulting to Johnson titled "All Coons Look Alike to Me." However, Rex Beach, who was there wrote: "A brass band climbed into the ring and it was rumored that with a true delicacy of feeling it was about to play 'All Coons Look Alike to Me' but racial feeling was too high, perhaps, and they favored us with a selection of national airs..."[11] At 1:45 o'clock Billy Jordan, official announcer for the event, entered the ring and cleared it of photographers and reporters. He then introduced William Muldoon, veteran fight trainer and sports writer, who made a few brief remarks on the "one free state" in the Union and suggested that everyone stand up and give three cheers "with heart and soul" for the glorious state of Nevada and its Governor. The response was enthusiastic.[12]

After a few more selections form the band the crowd began to grow restless in the heat. Liquor was not allowed inside the arena; there was only lemonade to quench the thirst. Many sports were nursing hangovers from a riotous night on the town and the music and the waiting did not improve their mood. Then Billy Jordan entered the ring again and began the introductions of the great and near great, and the mood of the crowd improved, sensing the great moment was at hand. First to be introduced was John L. Sullivan, and the crowd gave him a wild ovation. Then came "Gentleman" Jim Corbett, Tommy Burns, Bob Fitzsimmons, Tom Sharkey, Stanly Ketchel, Battling Nelson, Abe Attel, and Sam Langford. With the introductions finished, Tex Rickard entered the ring wearing a straw hat (to protect his head from the sun), took off his coat, rolled up his shirt sleeves, and walked the four corners as the crowd cheered. Rickard would be the official referee, and Charles White, substitute referee, if one were needed. Official time-keeper was George Harting. Timekeeper for Jeffries was Billy Gallagher, and timekeeper for Johnson, Stanley Ketchel. In Jeffries' corner were Jim Corbett, DeWitt Van Court, Jack Jeffries (his brother), Joe Choynski, Farmer Burns, Bob Armstrong, and Tod Boyer. In Johnson's corner were Billy Delaney, Sig Hart, Professor Burns, Doc Furey, and Al Kaufman.

All over the nation attention was focused on the fight. In large cities auditoriums had been rented and tickets sold where crowds could hear the latest telegraphic reports or witness imaginative facsimiles of the contest. In San Francisco, a regulation prize ring had been built on the stage of the Auditorium. A referee and two boxers dressed to represent Johnson and Jeffries re-enacted the fight blow-for-blow from telegraphic dispatches. Advertisements for the show read: "The reproduction will have all the thrill and excitement of the battle at Reno, without the discomfort, heat and expense. Every detail of the big fight will be vividly duplicated. Don't miss it. Bring your wife, your sweetheart or your chum and enjoy yourself." [13] In Kansas City, a crowd of 14,000 gathered in Convention Hall heard the fight described by roving announcers shouting through megaphones. On Long Island, a group gathered at the exclusive Edgemere Club, where William Vanderbelt, Howard Gould, Lawrence Drake and others followed the fight through a leased newswire of the *New York Times*. In Chicago at the Colosseum, an overflow crowd that included many black people watched illuminated electrical figures nine feet tall re-enact every blow on a huge electrical screen. In Hutchinson, Kansas at the Colored Holiness Church the pastor announced the church would hold special services during the fight to pray for Johnson's victory.

At 2:35 o'clock Jack Johnson entered the ring and was presented as the heavyweight champion of the world. There was a ripple of applause and a few catcalls. But Johnson smiled and waved to the crowd, beaming confidence. He tossed his gray silk robe to a second and flexed his arms above his head. He wore blue trunks and an American flag entwined around his waist. He weighed a trim 209 pounds, his head was shaved, he was 32 years old, just over six feet tall, waist 30 inches, with a reach of 72 inches. Then Jeffries and his seconds entered, much like a king with his retinue, Jim Corbett leading the way. The crowd stood on its feet and roared. Johnson, in his corner, clapped and cheered with the crowd. Jeffries wore purple trunks and an American flag threaded through the loops of his trunks. His weight was not given, but estimated at around 225 pounds, remarkable considering he had weighed over three hundred pounds six months before. He was 35 years old, an inch taller than Johnson, with a barrel chest that measured 43 inches when expanded, waist 35 inches, and a reach of 75 inches. He was larger and heavier than Johnson, huge by any standard, with a fierce countenance. If one were to judge solely by appearance, Jeffries certainly looked like a winner. Sports writers had called him a grizzly bear, a bull, and Jack London had tagged him "the abysmal brute." Jeffries folded his arms across his chest and stomped the canvas with his feet, his broad shoulders and powerful torso glinting in the sunlight. He gazed out over the vast arena, turning slowly, and the

crowd roared its approval of the "white hope." Jeffries shot a ferocious glance toward Johnson, but Johnson had turned his back, and
some said Johnson was too yellow to look into his opponent's face.
Harry Carr, a sports writer for the *Los Angeles Times* wrote: "I never
saw any human soul [meaning Johnson] so shaken with fear. When
the fight began Johnson was so frightened that his face was deathly,
ashen gray. His lips were dry and his eyes were staring with a sort of
horrified terror." [14] This was pure wishful thinking on Carr's part; actually, Johnson was flashing his golden smile at the crowd and if he
appeared ashen it was because he had a mild sunburn. Rickard sum-
moned the two fighters to the center of the ring and recited the
usual rules. Jeffries chewed gum rapidly and glared at Johnson.
Johnson smiled, balancing his weight from one foot to another.
They did not shake hands as they turned for their respective corners. The bell rang.

FIRST ROUND. Jeffries took the offensive, rushing at
Johnson from his famous crouch position. Johnson moved like a
dancer, avoiding the opening rushes with an economy of movement. Every time Jeffries rushed the crowd yelled, believing he
would pin Johnson against the ropes and deliver the knockout
punch, but Johnson danced away. They circled each other for ten
seconds looking for an opening. Johnson led with a left which
landed lightly on Jeffries' nose, Jeffries pushing against Johnson with
his weight advantage. Jeffries feinted a right and Johnson stood on
his toes and pushed Jeffries back with his left, then followed with a
left to the jaw, which did little damage. They clinched, Jeffries doing most of the clinching. When they broke, Jeffries aimed two
harmless lefts to the face, both slipped by Johnson, each merely
grazing his cheek. In Jeffries' corner, Corbett shouted at Johnson:
"Why don't you laugh?" Johnson winked and smiled back at
Corbett. They sparred and Jeffries tried to land with his left but
Johnson blocked. Jeffries clinched again, their arms locked, and

Jeffries used his weight to push Johnson around. As they broke, Johnson got in a left which grazed Jeffries' chin. They clinched again and were still in a clinch when the bell rang the end of the round. Johnson playfully tapped Jeffries on the shoulder and walked to his corner, smiling. It was an uneventful round, each man feeling out his opponent, both cautious.

SECOND ROUND. Johnson bounced up from his corner, chattering like a magpie. Corbett yelled at Johnson: "He wants to fight a little bit" – meaning Jeffries wanted to mix it up. Johnson answered back: "You bet I do, Mister Corbett." They sparred, to no effect, until Johnson darted in and landed twice on Jeffries' chin. The second blow was harder than the first, but Jeffries did not flinch. A clinch followed, and as they moved in a circle Johnson threw up his right and caught Jeffries on the chin. Rickard moved in and broke the clinch. As they separated, Jeffries swung a right to the stomach, but Johnson answered with two left uppercuts to the jaw. They clinched again. Both men were careful in breaking away. Jeffries went into his crouch but Johnson shot a right to the eye which landed, causing it to smart and water. The bell rang. Corbett and Johnson kept up their exchange of taunting remarks as the round ended.

THIRD ROUND. Johnson came up grinning: "Come in Jim," he said to Jeffries, feinting with his left. Jeffries swung a right to Johnson's stomach but missed. They clinched, breast to breast, and Johnson came up sharply with a left to Jeffries' nose. He followed quickly with another left to the face and a right to the jaw. Johnson showed that he was better at judging distance than Jeffries, and clearly the better man in close-in fighting. Johnson neatly blocked Jeffries' rushes or danced out of range. Corbett shouted caustic remarks at Johnson and Johnson answered back. Jeffries was taking punches but did not seem worried, though his face was flushed and covered with sweat. He gave Johnson a menacing look and tried to uppercut him but the blow went wide as Johnson dodged. At that point Johnson's grin was so wide it was visible to everyone in the arena. Johnson jabbed Jeffries in the face repeatedly and connected with an uppercut that drove Jeffries' head back. A clinch followed, and Johnson shot two blows to the head. On the break, Jeffries rushed in but Johnson blocked and Jeffries pushed him to the northwest corner of the ring. As the bell rang Johnson again tapped Jeffries lightly on the shoulder, smiling as he walked to his corner. Jeffries appeared nonchalant as he sat down in his corner, but it was clearly Johnson's round on points.

FOURTH ROUND. Jeffries missed with a left and Johnson answered with a glancing blow to Jeffries' ear. They clinched, and Johnson joked with Jeffries: "Don't rush, Jim. Don't you hear what I'm telling you?" – and backed it up with a right uppercut to the jaw. Rickard admonished Johnson that this was a boxing match and not a talkfest. Jeffries led and caught Johnson with a right on the chin, and blood trickled from Johnson's mouth. The crowd yelled: "First blood for Jeff!" – and they were on their feet. But the blow had not cut Johnson's lip, rather it had opened the cut when George Cotton had hit him during their exhibition match a few days earlier. Jeffries had done no damage, save start the bleeding. Corbett thought Jeffries now had the advantage and tried to rattle Johnson with twits and catcalls. Johnson answered with a right to Jeffries' jaw, followed with a hard right to the eye, snapping his head back sharply. In the clinch that followed Johnson asked Jeffries what had happened to those powerful punches he was famous for, then caught him with a hard left on the jaw. Jeffries forced Johnson against the ropes and tried several short-arm body punches, some of which found their mark but did no harm. Johnson replied with a right to the jaw which Jeffries shrugged off. While he was being cooled off in his corner, Johnson leaned over toward John L. Sullivan at ringside and said Jeffries couldn't hit hard.

FIFTH ROUND. Jeffries came out of his corner in a low crouch. Johnson feinted as Jeffries stepped away. Johnson said in a clear voice: "I will straighten him up in a minute." Those near ringside heard this and shouted back: "He will straighten you up, nigger." Jeffries landed two weak blows to the midsection and they clinched, as Johnson looked at Corbett and winked. Johnson hooked a left and cut Jeffries' upper lip. Jeffries led with his right but it was short, misjudging the distance. Johnson connected with a right to the jaw and followed with a combination to the forehead. Johnson jarred Jeffries with a straight left on the chin. Both men were bleeding from the mouth. Johnson slipped Jeffries' lead and he seemed annoyed because he couldn't find an opening through Johnson's defense. As they clinched, and as they broke Jeffries crouched again, then jumped to his toes and landed a straight left to the face as the bell rang. Johnson gave his customary tap on Jeffries' shoulder, and Corbett shouted from the corner: "Don't try to be friendly." Johnson smiled as he sat down in his corner, but Jeffries' face, as it was sponged by seconds, was grim and menacing.

SIXTH ROUND. "I'm going to mix with him now," Jeffries said to his seconds as the bell rang. They moved to the center of the ring and Johnson led with a hard right to the body. He followed with a left to the cheek, which opened a scab on Jeffries' face, drawing blood. Johnson shot a left to the stomach. A ringside fan asked Johnson if he wanted a drink. "Not now," he replied, "too much on hand now," and caught Jeffries with three rapid uppercuts to the jaw. They sparred, both fighters blocking and moving away. Johnson showed all the skill in judging his opponent. In the next exchange, Johnson shot a straight left to the jaw as Jeffries attempted to rush him, a walloping hard punch, the hardest blow of the fight. The pace of the fight quickened but Johnson's blows were faster and found their mark. In the clinch that followed, Johnson worked his short-arm punches to the head and body while Jeffries covered.

They broke, Jeffries rushed in but was caught by a wicked left uppercut that closed his right eye. Johnson danced away, grinned at Corbett, and shot a combination to Jeffries' nose, both connected. Jeffries was bleeding from his nose and chin, his hurt right eye badly discolored. As the round ended, Jeffries walked back to his corner rubbing his eye with his glove. His seconds worked frantically over his eye, but Jeffries seemed annoyed with their efforts and shook his head, as though trying to clear it.

SEVENTH ROUND. As Jeffries cautiously approached Johnson, his right eye nearly closed, it was clear to everyone he had respect for Johnson's ability to hit hard. "Come on, Jeff," Johnson taunted. They circled each other, and as Jeffries moved forward, Johnson danced back, shooting out his left. Jeffries rushed and threw a left but it glanced off Johnson's neck. A clinch followed and Rickard told them to break. Rickard had had little to do up to this point other than separate clinches, as both boxers were fighting fairly and no cautions had been given. In the next exchange, Johnson landed a terrific left on Jeffries' chin, followed by a right cross. Jeffries was beginning to show the effects of the punishment he had taken. The hot afternoon sun beat down on the boxers and both perspired freely, Jeffries sweating from almost every pore in his body. In a clinch again, Johnson drove his arms like pistons into Jeffries' damaged face. Johnson patted him on the back as the bell rang. As Johnson was sponged and rubbed, Corbett tried to rattle Johnson with verbal barbs. Johnson answered him from across the ring: "It's too late now to do anything, Jim. Your man is all in."

EIGHTH ROUND. Johnson waited for Jeffries to advance, and when he led, Johnson worried him with straight lefts to his chest. Jeffries led again and Johnson scored with a right to his ear and a hard left to the face. In the next exchange, Johnson landed a terrific straight punch to Jeffries' nose. "Hello, Corbett," Johnson said, "did you see that one?" Corbett clenched his teeth and did not answer. Jeffries managed to land a hard body blow to Johnson's mid-section but it did not faze him. A clinch followed. Johnson looked over Jeffries' shoulder and winked at the sports writers, keeping his left busy pounding Jeffries' body. Rickard separated them. Jeffries tried a left to the head but Johnson danced away, came in just as quickly and caught Jeffries on the chin. They clinched, circled around the ring, Jeffries holding Johnson and Johnson holding Jeffries, each trying to land punches in the in-fighting. No damage was done to either man during the close fighting. When the bell rang they were still clinching.

NINTH ROUND. Jeffries landed a weak left to the body and they went into a clinch. Johnson led on the break with a glancing blow to the cheek. He followed with a left to Jeffries' chin and a right to the jaw. All the while Johnson kept chattering and winking at Corbett. Jeffries butted with his head and delivered a right to Johnson's stomach. Johnson stepped back and bowed from the waist to the crowd. In the next exchange, Johnson shot a right to the stomach and Jeffries clinched. On the break, Johnson led with a left to the face but it only grazed the chin, and Jeffries stepped back. Jeffries crouched, and Johnson drove in a wicked left full to the stomach. Two straight lefts landed on Jeffries' mouth and eye, giv-ing him pause. Jeffries threw another hard right to the stomach, causing Johnson to grin. Johnson stepped in quickly and shot a left to his stomach, giving tit for tat. As the round ended, Jeffries' face was bleeding from several cuts. Johnson, by contrast, appeared fresh and talkative.

TENTH ROUND. The round started slowly, Jeffries moving out of Johnson's range. Johnson tried a left but Jeffries stepped back. Johnson moved quickly and shot two lefts to the head, followed by a right to the ear. Jeffries tried a counterpunch, to no effect. As Jeffries tried to come in, Johnson landed a straight right to the face, a hard blow that Jeffries walked straight into. A long clinch followed with considerable in-fighting. Johnson scored most of the blows, effective with his short-arm punches, driving upward with his left and right and landing on Jeffries' face. At one point Johnson whipped two lefts to the jaw and a right uppercut that forced his head back sharply, and Jeffries was heard to cry out, "Oh." They clinched again and Jeffries appeared sluggish as he waltzed with Johnson in the center of the ring. Jeffries' handlers in his corner looked worried as the round ended. One of Johnson's seconds asked Rickard to watch the gloves when the men were holding in a clinch to see they had not split or broken.

ELEVENTH ROUND. Jeffries looked for an opening but Johnson gave none. Johnson landed a light left on the cheek and Jeffries clinched. In the clinch, Johnson connected with a hard right to the chin. Jeffries broke, but Johnson was on top of him, hitting him with lefts and rights. Jeffries attempted to rush but Johnson side-stepped. The crowd mistakenly thought Jeffries was about to rally and cheered him with each new rush. But Johnson's form and strategy improved all the while, and his judgment of distance was perfect. Jeffries, on the other hand, was rushing but landing few punches, his judgment of distance hopeless and getting worse. He was spitting blood and breathing heavily. In every clinch Johnson scored with lefts and rights and uppercuts. As they broke from a clinch, Johnson caught Jeffries with a terrific left and turned his head clear around. Johnson was landing almost at will, his timing masterful, making it all look easy except to those few who knew what great skill lay behind every blow. Johnson glanced over at Corbett and said: "What do you think of this one, Jim?" – and shot a straight right to the chin that made Jeffries wobble. Corbett had grown silent and did not answer. Jeffries put his gloves up to the sides of his head and covered, but Johnson caught him a hard left on his bleeding mouth. Jeffries tried to rally again and the crowd cheered him on, but he landed only two weak blows. Incredibly, some sports writers called this round even, though Jeffries walked to his corner battered and bleeding. An old hand like John L. Sullivan knew better. He said it was all Johnson's round.

TWELFTH ROUND. Jeffries could not get Johnson's measure, and he tried to feint, and each time he did Johnson caught him on the face with a left or a right. In the clinches, Jeffries continued to hug, trying to buy time, while Johnson punished his face. Jeffries was visibly tiring. Once he rushed in but Johnson caught him on the jaw with a right uppercut. Jeffries crouched, tried two blows to the body but could not penetrate Johnson's defense. As Jeffries backed away, Johnson shot a straight left to the chin and drove Jeffries' head back sharply, followed with a flurry of lefts and rights. They clinched again and Johnson scored with a left and right to the face. Jeffries' seconds were tense and quiet as he walked back to his corner, spitting blood. Johnson's corner hummed with excitement and optimism as his seconds sponged water over his body.

THIRTEENTH ROUND. Jeffries walked slowly towards Johnson and tried a left, which resulted in a clinch. Johnson looked over Jeffries' shoulder and called out greetings to a few friends in the crowd. Jeffries moved awkwardly, missing a blow to the body. Johnson drove a left to his nose followed by a right cross to the face. Johnson unleashed a flurry of lefts and they landed where he aimed them, all on Jeffries' face. In the clinches that followed, Jeffries aimed a left to the body and Johnson made no effort to dodge the punch aimed at his ribs, as it carried no power. Johnson caught Jeffries on his chin with a right uppercut that seemed to lift him from the floor. Jeffries weakened at this moment. According to John L. Sullivan, it was the beginning of the end. Johnson landed a right and left on the face, Jeffries clinched but Johnson continued to pound away at him. His face bleeding in several places, one eye hugely swollen, Jeffries seemed to be having trouble locating Johnson. His hands were held too low, his arms bent slightly at the elbows. Johnson shot two more lefts and they connected with Jeffries' face. Corbett yelled to Jeffries from the corner to cover up and stay away from Johnson. He seemed to stare blankly at Corbett as the bell rang. He sat on his stool hunched over and refused to take encouragement from his seconds.

FOURTEENTH ROUND. Johnson led with his left and scored, another left hit Jeffries' mouth. In the clinch, Jeffries tried a right to the jaw where it landed lightly, doing no harm. Jeffries tried another right but Johnson danced away. Jeffries stood erect, the crowd yelled encouragement, and he aimed a straight left to the face where it connected, but without much force. Johnson stood back, grinned, and stuck out his stomach. "Ain't that a nice belly, Jeff? Why don't you hit it?" They closed in, Corbett yelled to Jeffries to watch out for uppercuts. Jeffries clinched and seemed to be gathering his legendary strength for a mighty blow when Johnson simply pushed him away and landed twice on his face with his left. "Why don't you fight?" yelled Corbett to Johnson. "I'm too clever – too much like you," Johnson snapped back, sending in four rapid-fire lefts to Jeffries' mouth, causing Jeffries to shake his head. During the break only water was used in Johnson's corner and towels to fan him with. In Jeffries' corner they used everything they had.

FIFTEENTH ROUND. As the round began it was clear that Jeffries was in trouble. One eye was closed, his face swollen and bleeding, and his strength was gone. Johnson waited for him to come in and then pummeled his face with left and right jabs. Jeffries tried to clinch but Johnson broke away and shot a left from his hip squarely into Jeffries' face. Jeffries staggered back against the ropes, his defenses down. Johnson was on him like a big cat, raining lefts and rights and Jeffries went down for the first time in his ring career. Timekeeper George Harting was yelling out the count at the top of his voice. Johnson walked around the center of the ring watching his opponent. Jeffries, resting on his haunches and right elbow, looked around with a dazed expression and slowly rose at the count of nine. Johnson stepped in as Jeffries straightened and shot another left full to the face. Jeffries reeled, tried to clinch but failed, and fell through the ropes on the south side of the ring. Several of his seconds and some sports writers got him back into the ring again and he slowly rose to his feet at the count of nine. It was at this point that Jeffries' friends called for Rickard to stop the fight. "Stop it! Stop it," they shouted from all sides. "Don't let him be knocked out!" But Rickard paid no attention to these appeals. Jeffries staggered over to the east side of the ring and Johnson stepped into him and sent him reeling with a right to the head and a left to the nose. Jeffries was helpless now, groggy and bloody. He went down a third time, sprawling over the lower rope, half out of the ring. The crowd was on its feet, some yelling, some cheering. Johnson walked around the ring, watching the timekeeper raise and lower his arms with the count. Between the count of seven and eight one of Jeffries' seconds broke into the ring, followed by two more, and this transgression of the rules ended the fight. Billy Delaney, Johnson's chief handler, broke through the ropes and demanded Rickard declare Johnson the winner. Rickard, yelling at the top of his voice to make himself heard, said he had already declared Johnson the winner. Rickard then placed his hand on Johnson's shoulder and declared him the winner. Although Jeffries was not officially counted out, it was clear to everyone he could not have got to his feet before the count of ten. Johnson stood in the center of the ring and was hugged by Delaney and his seconds. Johnson was flushed with the excitement of victory but breathing regularly. Jeffries was dragged to his corner by his seconds, who set to work on him. Johnson walked to Jeffries' corner – probably to shake hands – but the congestion in the ring was so great with officials and police he could not move, and when Corbett saw him he waved him away. The first man to congratulate Johnson in his corner was John L. Sullivan. Johnson left the ring quickly with a police escort. When his seconds had got him partially revived and the bleeding checked, Jeffries was taken to Moana Springs. People swarmed into the ring and began tearing it to pieces for souvenirs. Within five minutes, canvas, ropes, and anything not nailed down had disappeared.

    *   *   *

  Jeffries' disadvantage lay in the fact that he had retired six years before and had not fought since. His retirement had been real. As a boxer, Jeffries had never been noted for his quickness or clever skills. He had won in the past through his great strength and recuperative powers. Jeffries tried again and again to break through Johnson's defenses and failed. He crouched, feinted and hit, but he was too slow. Each time he hit with all his power, Johnson danced away with an agility that was astonishing. When he did hit Johnson, it was not the old Jeffries, and he never hurt him. Jeffries was not the same man that had fought Tom Sharkey for twenty-five rounds in 1899 and won – nor the same man who had knocked out former champion Bob Fitzsimmons. He had lost his ability to hit hard, as Johnson remarked to John L. Sullivan at the end of the fourth round.

  Johnson, on the other hand, was at the peak of his powers. Since his fight with Tommy Burns in 1908 he had trained hard, developed his skills to an art. He had the ability to hit hard, with both his left and right, and his defensive skills were so great it was almost impossible to hit him. His coordination and quickness of response were remarkable. Only a few besides Johnson knew this, as most had focused their attention on Jeffries. It was also widely thought – because of reports in the press – that Johnson had a "yellow streak." And that he could not deliver a hard punch with his left. But these notions were quickly dispelled as the fight proceeded, and even his severest critics had to admit they had been wrong. Johnson gave a statement to the Associated Press after the fight in which he said he had been confident of winning even before he entered the ring. Jeffries' blows had no power behind them, he said, and he felt he had outclassed him in every way. When Jeffries seemed to land body blows, spectators at ringside thought they had landed, but Johnson said he had blocked them with his glove. "I am unmarked," he said, "and in shape to do battle again tomorrow if it were necessary." He said Jeffries fought a game fight, that he kept coming at him with the heart of a true fighter, and that no man could say he did not do his best. "There was nothing said between us which was rough. He joked me and I joked him. I told him he was a bear, but I was a gorilla and would defeat him." When asked if he would accept the challenge by Sam Langford to fight the winner, Johnson replied that no attention would be given it, that Langford couldn't give him a fight that would draw a big enough gate.[15]

A statement he gave to the *San Francisco Examiner* gave further insights into the fight. The blow that ended the fight, Johnson said, was a right to the jaw, but the right was only a follower to a left cross which caught Jeffries on the jaw. Jeffries was hit hard by the first blow, and when the second was landed an instant later, he had to go down. Johnson said before the fight many sports writers had said he had no punch. "Well, I think today's exhibition of punching should send that story to the waste basket, along with the 'yellow streak' fable." As for comments that he ran away from Jeffries in the ring, hoping to tire him out, he said that he never ran away from anybody, that a champion running away from a fight would make a sorry spectacle. He said he had landed the first blow in the fight, kept on leading and landing, and had landed ten to Jeffries' one. "I had a lot of fun with Jim Corbett while today's fight was going on," Johnson said. "He shouted to Jeffries this afternoon, 'He will show the yellow soon.' I answered over Jeffries' shoulder: 'Well, he made you show, and if he makes me quit I'll come over there and get you. That will make us even.'"[16]

Later that afternoon, Jeffries gave a statement to the press. He had been lifted from the ring, carried to an automobile, and driven back to Moana Springs. He said he remembered nothing of the drive back. When he finally regained his senses and his mind cleared, he was sitting in a chair on the lawn in front of his cottage, his brother Jack, looking anxious, working to revive him.[17] A week or so before, plans had been made for a gala victory dinner at the Hotel Golden. On the other hand, if he lost, a simple farewell dinner for close friends would be held at Moana Springs. Corbett and others had seen to the arrangements and the table had been set for twenty-five guests. When the dinner was served, fifteen chairs were vacant. His fair-weathered friends had abandoned him. Some had lost so much money betting on him they chose to forget him as soon as possible. As Jeffries said: "It did not take long to find out who my real friends were after my downfall. The real ones were there, trying to cheer me up and show me they were loyal and, after all, that is the only kind worth while."[18] Jeffries explained to the press that he had lost the fight because he no longer had the strength and vigor of youth. "The things I used to do were impossible. For instance, I used to shoot in a right-hand body punch, a short-range body blow that never failed me. When I tried it today, the snap wasn't there and it was only a love tap." He said it wouldn't have made any difference had he boxed more with his sparring partners, or trained harder. "I guess it's all my own fault. I was getting along nicely and living peacefully on my alfalfa farm, but when they started calling for me and mentioning me as the 'white hope,' I guess my pride got the better of my judgment. I worked long and hard to condition myself, and I was fit, as far as my strength goes, but the old snap and dash were not with me. Six years ago the result might have been different. But now – well, I guess the public will leave me alone after this."[19]

Tex Rickard commented that Johnson was the most wonderful fighter that ever pulled on a glove. Johnson was never in danger, and did as he pleased with Jeffries. Rickard said he felt sorry for the big white man as he was hammered by Johnson's blows, that it was a pitiable sight. Rickard confessed that before the fight he had thought Jeffries would win. "The fight was won and lost when Jeffries went through the ropes the first time. This is official. The other knockdown does not count. It was this way: Jeffries was brought to his knees and as he arose, dazed, Johnson hit him with a succession of lefts that sent him through the ropes. As he lay there several of his seconds caught hold of him and helped him to his feet. Under the rules of the game, which I have read thoroughly while certain people were saying that I couldn't referee a fight, this disqualified Jeffries, and Johnson was the winner."[20]

Jack London filed his final story from Reno after the fight was over. He said Johnson fought a white man, in the white man's country, before a white man's audience, and the audience was a Jeffries' audience, and he won. "The greatest battle of the century was a monologue delivered to twenty thousand spectators by a smiling Negro, who was never in doubt and who was never serious for more than a moment at a time," he wrote. He said Johnson never extended himself during the fight; he didn't have to. Jeffries never had Johnson in trouble, that no blow he landed ever hurt Johnson. "Johnson came out of the fight practically undamaged," he concluded.[21]

Rex Beach, who had reported the Gans-Herman fight in Tonopah in 1907, and who had an ambivalent attitude toward the sport of boxing, wrote: "Some 15,000 of us went out and broiled in the sun to see a great prize fight, and while it was great from the point of view of a spectacle and from the courage displayed, it was really no fight at all." Instead, he wrote that it was a pitiful tragedy, in the sense that everyone had expected to see the old Jeffries, not realizing that time had taken its toll on the man. "We saw but the shell of a man, fair to the eye and awe-inspiring in his shape, to be sure, but empty of youth's vigor. The years had done their work...and so he lost." Beach went on to say that he doubted if Jeffries, in his prime, could have defeated Johnson, so masterful was his performance, so marvelous his speed. "He demonstrated further that his race has acquired full stature as men...He fought carefully, fearlessly, intelligently. There remains no living man to dispute his title. And there seems little likelihood it will ever be taken from him. If such a thing should come to pass it will be because time has robbed him of that fierce and blazing energy that lurks deep in his being, as Jeff was robbed, in the night."[22]

On his way to the railroad station that evening to catch the train for Chicago, Johnson and Etta were recognized in their open touring car. Johnson had the driver slow down so he could talk to his admirers. As their car passed by the Hotel Golden, Rex Beach happened to look out the window at that moment:

Just now an automobile paused below my window and Jack Johnson, Heavyweight Champion of the World, was in it. He had no mark upon his person as he bowed his thanks to the bellowed greetings offered him. The last picture I have is of a giant black man shaking the hand of a newsboy as he runs beside the champion's motor car, with a surging mass of humanity behind.[23]

AFTERWORD

In Reno there were no riots after the fight. The sports accepted the outcome stoically, much as they would a losing bet on the turn of a card. They paid off or collected their bets and headed for the railway yards. By morning all the train specials had departed, leaving the yards deserted. The streets were swept clean, the mining men moved back into the Hotel Golden, and life in Reno returned to normal.

But it was not so in other parts of the country. As soon as the wire services reported that Johnson had defeated Jeffries, trouble broke out. Jubilant blacks shot firecrackers in the streets and fired pistols into the air as resentful whites watched. Liquor made an already tense situation worse, and saloons were often the flashpoint for trouble. In cities and towns across the nation riots erupted. The worst were in New York City. One black man was rescued by police from an angry crowd of white men who had a rope around his neck, ready to lynch him from a lamp post. Another black man, chased by a mob from Lincoln Park to Central Park, was given sanctuary by a doctor who took him into his house and defied the mob with a loaded revolver. The black man's skull had been split open and he was rushed to a hospital. Between Thirty-Seventh and Thirty-Ninth streets, a mob of more than one thousand whites roamed at will, kicking and beating any black man they could catch. When the ticker-tape in a saloon on Eighth Avenue announced that Johnson had won, a crowd of about fifty whites ran into the street shouting, "Let's lynch the first Negro we see." At that moment a streetcar came along and they spied a black man in one of the seats reading a newspaper. They climbed on the car and began beating the black. A policeman forced his way aboard and arrested two white men, who were kicking the black man. Someone fired a revolver and within minutes an ugly crowd had surrounded the trolley. Another policeman arrived as the mob tried to take the two arrested whites from police custody, and the two policemen were shoved off the trolley. Luckily, a patrol wagon arrived with fifteen policemen and the mob was dispersed. A gang of whites known as the "Hounds of Hell" took possession of another section of Eighth Avenue near 130th Street and held the ground against efforts of many police to remove them. This mob held three blacks, all badly beaten, ready to hang them from the nearest lamp post. Several mounted police arrived and drove their horses in a flying wedge into the mob and rescued the blacks, one of whom was unconscious. In another part of New York City, a black man stopped at a newsstand to buy a newspaper. White men grabbed the paper from him, asked him what he thought of the fight, and when he gave a noncommittal reply, they beat him so badly that he required nine stitches to close a gash on his head. There were riots through the night in the San Juan Hills district, where police were posted on the roofs of buildings on every block. One group of fifty blacks who were out celebrating Johnson's victory fired pistol shots into the air as they made their way to San Juan Hill. They were quickly broken up by police who had set up headquarters in a nearby park. In a few instances, rowdy blacks contributed to the trouble. Two blacks at-tacked two whites in front of a building on West Thirty-Sixth Street. When chased by the police, one fled into the building and up to the roof. When caught and handcuffed, the man's angry wife appeared on the roof brandishing a frying pan, which she aimed at one of the police. Below, an angry mob collected in the street, and when police appeared with their prisoners the mob attacked and beat several blacks gathered at the edge of the crowd. Some whites drew revolvers and used them as blackjacks. The two policemen had to beat their way with riot clubs through the mob, which de-manded the two blacks be turned over to them. But the police got them safely through and took them to the local precinct station. Riots continued through the night and into the early morning hours. One New York newspaper called it a "reign of terror" and when it was finally over six people were dead and dozens injured.

In Norfolk, Virginia, sailors from the Navy base roamed the streets beating blacks. Riots broke out in several districts. A detach-ment of marines was sent out to stop the rioting. In St. Joseph, Missouri, a white man attempted to defend a black man severely beaten by a mob and was himself attacked and beaten unconscious. There was rioting in Pueblo, Colorado, where a pitched battle was fought between blacks and whites. The entire police force of Pueblo was required to restore order. In Mounds, Illinois, a group of four blacks shot up the town and when a black constable attempted to stop them he was shot and killed. At Keystone, West Virginia, blacks were reported to hold the town hostage, police helpless to in-tervene. Telephone and telegraph connections to Keystone had been cut off. One black man was killed in Omaha, Nebraska. On a train between Little Rock and Iron Mountain, Arkansas, a railroad conductor was shot and wounded when he attempted to stop a fight between whites and blacks. A black man riding a trolley in Houston, Texas, who was loudly proclaiming Johnson's victory to his fellow passengers, had his throat cut by a white man. He nearly bled to death before he reached a hospital. In Atlanta, Georgia, police acted swiftly to prevent a riot downtown when they arrested a dozen whites and several blacks and set up police barricades in the streets. There was a gunfight at Uvaldia, Georgia, which left three people dead and scores wounded. Bad as it was, the violence was not pandemic. In Chicago, with its large black population, the mood was one of celebration, not violence. Los Angeles and San Francisco received the news calmly, as did Denver, Kansas City, St. Louis, Seattle, Portland, Philadelphia, and many other cities and towns.

Social reformers had unwittingly laid the groundwork for violence when they ignored the issue of equality. They saw the fight simply as an exercise in bloodletting and brutality. The idea that a black man might have a fair chance to win through his ability in the white man's arena – if not in the broad landscape of American life – was to admit equality of a sort, and this was the root of all objections, whether realized or not. To deny a black man entry into the white man's arena was to practice discrimination, and nothing else. The idea of equality, when it was discussed, was offensively stated: "We believe the notion of equality both between the races and the individuals is absolutely ridiculous."[1] And so the fight was seen instead as one of racial superiority of white against black in an atavistic struggle for supremacy, devoid of intelligence. Others had done their mischievous work, too; some editorial writers, especially those in the south, had written that if Johnson won, the result would be race war. Some politicians warned that a Johnson victory would go to the heads of blacks, give them uppity ways, and young black men who saw Johnson as a role model would crowd white women and white children off the sidewalks.

Newspapers deplored the riots and editorialized against them, but some remarks were more provocative than propitious. A dispatch from Fleet Street in London remarked: "The *Morning Post*

in London fears the triumph of Jack Johnson over Jeffries will be exploited all over the world in the interests of local sedition. [The
Morning Post] expresses the opinion that if the white man in the
United States has reason for the assertion of racial superiority and
– we believe he has good and sufficient reason – then in its incep-
tion the Jeffries-Johnson fight was a colossal blunder."[2] But the riots gave the reformers and politicians the ammunition they needed
to ban the fight film, saying that if it were shown in theaters across
the land more riots could be expected. Their efforts were eminently
successful: the film was banned by law in virtually every city and
town in the nation.

When Johnson was asked to comment on newspaper stories
that his victory had caused the race riots, he replied: "Why should
they bring in the black race against the white race in athletics? I
licked Tommy Burns fairly. I did the same in my fight with Jeffries.
My battle with Jeffries was not a contest between a black man and
a white man, but between two boxers who were out to establish their
right to the heavyweight championship of the world, a right I claimed
and Jeffries disputed. I beat him and now the matter is settled."[3]

*   *   *

Jeffries left Reno on the Owl Express for San Francisco and
Los Angeles, accompanied by his wife, brother Jack, and Sam
Berger. Jim Corbett left on the Overland Limited for New York for
a vaudeville engagement at the American Theater, where he would
entertain audiences with his version of the Johnson-Jeffries fight.
Curiously, Johnson had been engaged to appear at Hammerstein's
Theater for one week, scheduled to open the same night as Corbett,
only a few blocks away. In Oakland, there was a small crowd to
greet Jeffries when the Owl rolled in, most of them old friends, but
no celebration or brass band. From Oakland he traveled to Los

Angeles and went into seclusion at his alfalfa farm. The "white hope," upon whom the nation had fastened its attention, had fallen from grace, and perhaps no man ever fell as hard as Jeffries.

In the years following the fight at Reno, his life was as unspectacular as Johnson's was spectacular. On his ranch he raised thoroughbred cattle, alfalfa, and oranges. His saloon and restaurant in Los Angeles provided a modest income, though he was seldom seen there. His great love was hunting and fishing, and he was often gone for weeks on camping trips into the mountains. In 1921, he sold his herd of prize cattle, which he said was a rich man's luxury and one he could no longer afford. He invested the proceeds in oil wells and gold mines, which proved disastrous. He financed the drilling of three exploratory wells, all of them dry. Then mining engineers showed him charts and assay reports which looked marvelous on paper, promising big returns once the gold ore was struck. When they had finished with him, mining promoters had extracted from him a quarter of a million dollars – all his available cash – and got him to sign notes for assessment fees. There was no gold, of course. The notes came due and the promoters skipped in the dead of night leaving Jeffries holding the bag. The notes were called in and Jeffries had to declare bankruptcy. For the first time in his life he had no cash. But he still had the ranch, the saloon and restaurant. And then came an offer for a vaudeville tour with Tom Sharkey. The two men had scarcely seen each other over the years, and when they appeared on stage they were two middle-aged men with pot bellies, heads bald as a cucumber. The act opened with a song and dance routine, helped out by a line of chorus girls, Sharkey and Jeffries taking a twirl across the footlights with one or two of the girls. This was followed by three rounds of boxing. The tour opened at Loew's Theater in Buffalo, New York, and when the boxing started Sharkey landed a hard right on Jeffries' jaw and Jeffries drove punches into Sharkey's ribs. When the first round ended, the stage referee said to them: "What are you guys trying to do, kill each other? For God's sake ease up or the act won't last a week." After that they rehearsed and polished the act, pulling most of their punches. The public was delighted. As the tour moved across the country they were greeted by large crowds and packed houses. The public seemed to have forgotten the "white hope" who had lost to Johnson in 1910, and if they had not forgotten, they had forgiven. The tour helped put Jeffries back on his feet financially, and it proved a good tonic for his spirits. He went on the road again in 1927 with a touring circus, a life which he found amusing and interesting.[4]

Many people had definite opinions as to whether Jeffries had been "doped" before the fight with Johnson, including Jeffries himself. At first, he said not, not wanting to use it as an excuse for his defeat. But by 1929 when his biography was published, he had changed his mind on the subject. For several days before the fight, he wrote, he felt sluggish and listless. After his return to Los Angeles he complained he felt tired all the time and was unable to think clearly. When his condition did not improve, he consulted "one of the most prominent doctors in Los Angeles, a diagnostician of national repute" who made a series of tests. Blood tests determined, Jeffries wrote, that "my body was saturated with a drug which affects the brain and at the same time deadens the nerves that affects the muscles. I learned that the drug is one of the most powerful and slow acting of poisons that, if the patient is not treated promptly, it often results fatally."[5] Jeffries did not identify the poison by name but said it was known in athletics, where it was sometimes used for severe rheumatic cases to deaden pain. "From that day," he wrote, "we have never ceased our efforts to pin the guilt on those we believed were involved in the plot. Since then there never has been the slightest doubt in my mind but that I was 'slipped something,' thus far however we never have been able to get legal proof, or to learn when and how the drug was given to me."[6] Months of treatment were required, he said, to get the drug out of his system. But in 1927, according to a blood test, minute traces of it still remained. That would mean, according to Jeffries, the drug remained in his system for seventeen years, which seems an uncommonly long period. He said he made every effort to trace this drug but had failed, meaning that he had not connected any one person to the "plot" to dope him. Nevertheless, he speculated upon what might have happened, such as one time when he returned from road work, hot and tired, and was served a cup of tea at his training camp. "Absent-mindedly, I started to sip it. The odd thing about it is that during all my training I drank nothing; no tea, coffee, or even water, believing it slowed me up. Peculiarly too, we never as far as we can recall, had tea either at home or in training camp. I sipped at the tea and swallowed some, remarking that it tasted bitter, and thought nothing of it – at the time."[7] But if the tea contained the drug, he said, it was only one of several times he was doped. Another time, when he had left camp with friends at daybreak to go fishing on the Truckee River, they stopped at a wayside restaurant and ate breakfast. They had the cook prepare some sandwiches to take with them. The next morning, Jeffries said, he felt dull and drowsy.

At least three persons in Jeffries' camp could not be trusted, he said, because while telling him he was sure to win, they were actually placing large bets on Johnson to win. "We know that, the day before the fight, I was ten to seven favorite. At nine o'clock the night before the fight the gamblers suddenly started taking all the Jeffries money they could find. Telegrams went out to the big gamblers in every big city in the country, advising them to bet on Johnson...It is not yet too late to bring to justice the crooked gamblers and others who had a hand in this plot. I still have men working on the case and keeping steadily after legal evidence, and I will never cease trying to get to the bottom of the affair."[8]

If Jeffries' story stretches our credulity it is because it leaves too many questions unanswered. He never names the "poison" nor does he give the name of the doctor whom allegedly discovered the toxin in his blood. He could not identify the person or persons who "slipped something" to him, though presumably had men working on that problem for seventeen years. Then we are told he was doped not once but probably several times, once with a cup of tea at his training camp, another when he stopped at a restaurant for breakfast. Both stories are suspect, especially the one where he was served doped eggs for breakfast. How could the cook in the restaurant possibly have known Jeffries would stop there on that particular morning for breakfast? And if that person prepared doped sandwiches for his party, how was it that Jeffries happened to get the doped sandwich and the others did not? No one else in his party was doped. This is speculation of the worst kind, certainly not proof. And finally, Jeffries points his finger at "crooked gamblers and the others who had a hand in this plot." This would seem to infer that certain anonymous gamblers were in league with three men in his training camp who were suspect because they had bet on Johnson, a very broad generalization. Why did Jeffries change his mind and come to believe there was a plot or conspiracy to dope him? Probably because the first suggestion came from his own camp, when someone threw it out as a possible explanation for his sluggish performance in the ring. Sports writers picked up on it and the question was put before the public. After that, it gained the credulity common to all folklore, fed by the suspicion that something was fishy about the whole thing. Once it had made its way into folklore, Jeffries came to believe it. He concocted a story to support it – much as Johnson invented fanciful stories about himself for his autobiography – but his story gives no proof, only speculation. The truth of the matter about Jeffries' performance in the ring that day lies elsewhere. He was sluggish because he had not

fought in seven years, he had not taken his training at Reno seriously, and as he put it himself, he had lost the snap of youth.

In later years, Jeffries made occasional appearances at baseball games, where he acted as umpire or at boxing matches as referee. He was present at the Dempsey-Tunney fight in Chicago,
September 22, 1927, and was introduced to the crowd as one of
boxing's greats. In the 1940s, he converted part of his ranch into a
private picnic ground, which was popular with some of the
Hollywood movie studios. An old movie short for theater release
was shot there, narrated by Hedda Hopper, which shows a birthday
party given for child actress Jane Withers, with several dozen children as guests. During World War II, George Raft, the movie star,
organized and sponsored a Cavalcade of Sports show that toured
Army and Navy bases, putting on exhibitions of boxing and other
sporting events. It was somewhat like a touring USO show, except
that Raft paid all expenses out of his own pocket. Jeffries toured
with this show for a time and acted as referee for the boxing contests, but never in the ring as a boxer. In 1953, Jeffries died of natural causes at his ranch in Burbank, California, at age 78.

*   *   *

Jack Johnson was sitting on top of the world, or so it seemed.
He had defeated the "white hope." He had retained his crown of
world's heavyweight champion. The future seemed to offer a horizon of fabulous possibilities. He could arrange his future fights much
as he chose, sure of a large share of the purse. He could pick and
choose from offers of vaudeville tours, a few profitable investments,
and with one or two fights a year, fees from film rights, he might
earn as much as a quarter of a million a year. He could live like a
prince. As his train sped eastward across the Nevada desert toward
Ogden and Chicago, Johnson could not have imagined that what

the future held for him would be exactly the opposite of such great expectations. The first hint of trouble came at Ogden where a crowd of some five hundred had gathered to catch a glimpse of the champion. Johnson appeared briefly on the rear platform of his car and shook hands with a few who offered congratulations. He returned inside and had seated himself beside Etta when three roughnecks walked up to the window and began shouting obscene epithets. Johnson leaped to his feet but his manager restrained him. The roughnecks rushed to the rear of the coach and attempted to climb upon the observation platform. One was greeted with a foot in the face by one of Johnson's trainers, another was clubbed by a railroad detective, and the third received a mouthful of tobacco juice in his eyes. Police arrested the troublemakers and the train pulled out of the station. One fanciful report in an eastern newspaper said Johnson had been shot and killed by angry whites and that a million dollars in cash and gold had been found in his luggage.

When Johnson's train pulled into the Chicago and Northwestern station he received a tremendous ovation from the five thousand blacks gathered there to meet him. He made his way through the milling crowd, looming above them, clasping hands and smiling. Minutes later he was in his new racing car, speeding to his family home. His mother, Mrs. Tiny Johnson and members of his family, waited on the porch. As he pulled up, flags waved and a drum major struck up a costumed marching band and played "America," and "Mister Johnson, Turn Me Loose." Reporters asked Jack if he would fight Sam Langford next. "Let him come up with $20,000 and we might talk about it," he said. "What about the future?" a reporter asked. "Well, I have a contract for thirty weeks of vaudeville. And they want me to come to Europe," he answered. "I certainly would like to stay right here and I don't know but what I will, unless they force me out." Prophetic words.

Johnson went on to New York City to begin his vaudeville

engagement. When he arrived in Buffalo on the "Jack Johnson Special" he appeared on the platform and greeted the cheering crowd. This scene was repeated at each station until they reached Grand Central, where thousands of blacks thronged the streets, shooting off fireworks and cheering. The crowd was so dense that police had difficulty clearing a path for Johnson's party. This was perhaps the greatest moment for Johnson by way of public demonstration. As his car made its way to Herald Square – which was crowded to overflowing – it was surrounded by cheering blacks. The car stopped at the entrance to the Baron Wilkes Hotel, headquarters for the New York sporting crowd, and Johnson stood up, waving to the crowd. If the mayor did not show up to present Johnson with the key to the city, the public paid him tribute each night at Hammerstein's Theater when packed houses applauded his vaudeville performance.

While the search for another "white hope" continued, Johnson toured Europe with several vaudeville companies. He had tried to arrange a fight in England with Billy Wells, a popular heavyweight, but he had met with opposition again from the National Sporting Club and the London City Council. Back in the United States in 1912, Johnson was approached by Jack Curley, a rising fight promoter, who wanted to promote a return match between Johnson and Fireman Jim Flynn. Johnson had fought Flynn before in San Francisco on November 2, 1907. Johnson wondered if Flynn was a credible contender, whether the fight would attract a large crowd. Curley pointed out that Flynn had fought well for eleven rounds, until Johnson had found an opening and knocked him out. It had been two years since the Jeffries fight. Johnson had not trained much in the meantime, nor had Flynn. For some reason, the fight was scheduled to take place in the remote town of Las Vegas, New Mexico, which proved a mistake. It was too far from metropolitan centers, and railroad connections were difficult. Etta accompanied

The cartoonist may have thought the price for box seats exorbitant and those who rushed to buy them gullible. But all box seats had been sold in advance and on the day of the fight only scalpers offered them for sale. *Author's collection*

A cartoon-type post card issued for the fight. Featured among the spectators are a city slicker, cowboy, prospector, and (at right) Indian. *Paul Elcano Collection*

This widely circulated post card exploited the racial issue – which had nothing to do with the merits of either man's boxing ability. *Paul Elcano Collection*

Souvenir pennant from the Johnson-Jeffries fight in Reno, Nevada, July 4, 1910.
Rick Reviglio Collection

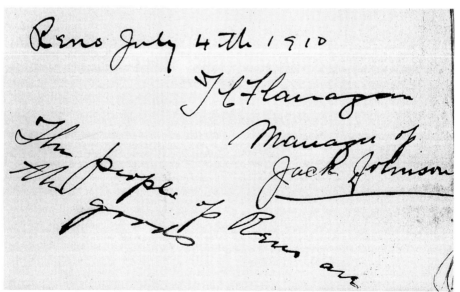

Sentiment written by Tex Rickard, Johnson-Jeffries fight referee, in the autograph album of Frank Golden Jr., July 6, 1910. *Nevada Historical Society*

Sentiment written by T. C. Flanagan, Jack Johnson's manager, in the autograph album of Frank Golden, Jr., Reno, July 4, 1910. *Nevada Historical Society*

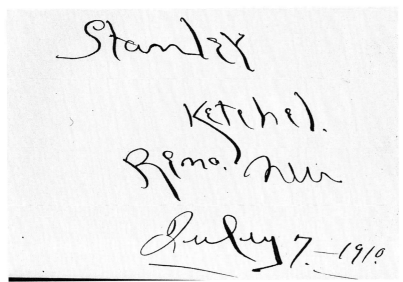

Signature of Stanley Ketchel in the autograph album of Frank Golden, Jr., Reno, Nevada, July 7, 1910. *Nevada Historical Society*

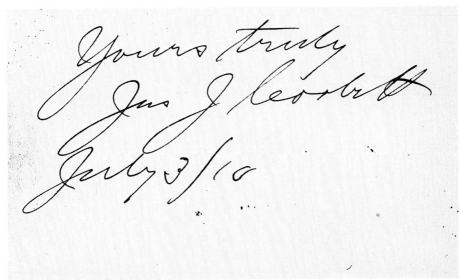

Signature of "Gentleman" Jim Corbett in the autograph album of Frank Golden, Jr., July 3, 1910. *Nevada Historical Society*

Caption reads: "Johnson and Wife. Reno, Nev." – which is an error, as Johnson was not married at the time. (Johnson married Etta Duryea, January 18, 1911.) The woman in the picture is Belle Schreiber, a companion, who would later testify against Johnson at his trial for violation of the Mann Act in 1913. The photograph was taken at Rick's Resort. *Author's collection*

Caption reads: "Johnson's Wife at Ringside" – an error, as Johnson had no wife at this time. The woman may be Belle Schreiber, to whom she bears a strong resemblance. It is definitely not Etta Duryea, who was also in Reno at the time, and whom Johnson would marry the following year. *Paul Elcano Collection*

No. 41. Mrs. Johnson Cheering the Champi[on]

There was no Mrs. Johnson at the time of the fight. Johnson did not marry until the following year. The woman is probably Belle Schreiber, who appears in another ringside photograph taken by Dana captioned: "Johnson's Wife at Ringside." *Paul Elcano Collection*

Billy Jordan, who acted as master-of-ceremonies at the fight, introduces Tex Rickard (right). Rickard was official referee for the fight. *Paul Elcano Collection*

Billy Jordan (right) introduces former heavyweight champion Bob Fitzsimmons (left). *Paul Elcano Collection*

Billy Jordan (hand raised) introduces Tom Sharkey (left) to the crowd, with John L. Sullivan (back to camera) in the background. *Paul Elcano Collection*

The great John L. Sullivan (left) is introduced to the crowd by Billy Jordan (right). The crowd gave Sullivan an enthusiastic ovation. *Paul Elcano Collection*

Billy Jordan (hand raised) introduces Frank Gotch, with Bob Fitzsimmons (far left) in the background. *Paul Elcano Collection*

Billy Jordan introduces Sam Langford (left) to the crowd, Langford hoped to fight the winner for the title but no such match was ever arranged. Langford, along with Sam McVey and Joe Jeanette, was one of the great black boxers at the time. *Paul Elcano Collection*

Billy Jordan introduces James Jeffries. *Courtesy J.P. Pinocchio, Pinocchio's Bar & Grill, Reno, Nevada.*

Billy Jordan (hand raised) introduces Jack Johnson. George Cotton and Sig Hart are at extreme left. *Paul Elcano Collection*

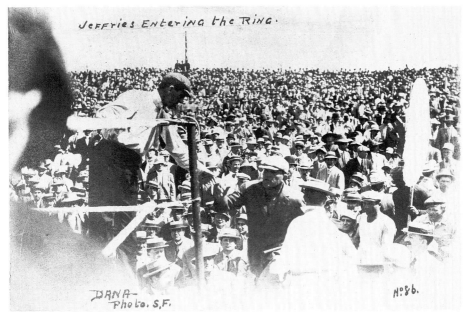

Jeffries entering the ring. He was dressed in a suit, wearing a cap. He wore his boxing trunks underneath his street clothes and changed shoes in the ring. *Paul Elcano Collection*

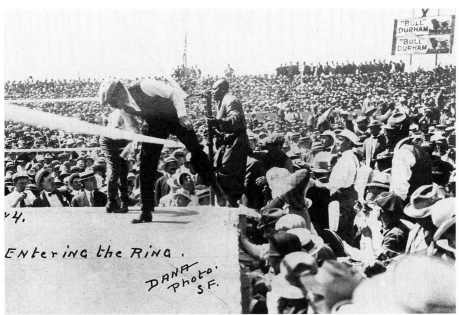

Jack Johnson entering the ring (wearing robe, with hand on ring post). *Paul Elcano Collection*

S. Johnson being introduced.

Jack Johnson (right) introduced to the crowd by Billy Jordan (center) with George Cotton at left. *Paul Elcano Collection*

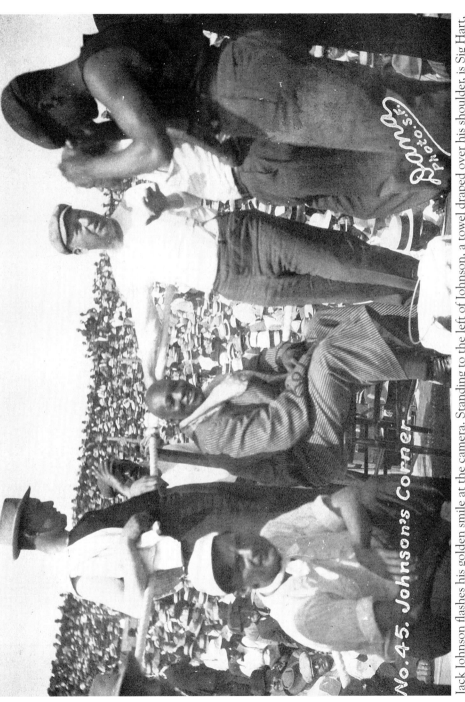

Jack Johnson flashes his golden smile at the camera. Standing to the left of Johnson, a towel draped over his shoulder, is Sig Hart, Johnson's manager. George Cotton (at right) appears to be drinking from a glass. *Paul Elcano Collection*

Round 1

Round 1. Jefferies took the offensive but Johnson blocked and danced away. There was much clinching as both men attempted to size up his opponent. *Paul Elcano Collection*

No. 66 Johnson-Jeffries

Jeffries in his famous crouch position from which he aimed a blow to the body of his opponent with all his weight behind it. This tactic had served him well against earlier opponents, but it was ineffective against Johnson.

Paul Elcano Collection

Round 3. Johnson connected with several hooks and an uppercut that drove Jeffries' head back. Jeffries could not land on Johnson, and toward the end of the round Johnson jabbed Jeffries in the face repeatedly. *Paul Elcano Collection*

Round 5 of the fight, during which Johnson connected with a left hook, cutting Jeffries' lip. *Paul Elcano Collection*

Round 9 of the fight, during which both men landed blows but did no real damage. *Paul Elcano Collection*

Round 10. There was much clinching in this round. Johnson was better than Jeffries at in-fighting and landed several hooks that hurt Jeffries. *Paul Elcano Collection*

Johnson talking to Corbett. Round 4. No 97.

During the fight former champion "Gentleman" Jim Corbett, who was in Jeffries' corner, taunted Johnson with remarks, and Johnson answered with his own. Jack London described this verbal exchange as the "second fight." Tex Rickard, referee, at right. *Paul Elcano Collection*

Round 12. Johnson scored with uppercuts and hooks, causing Jeffries to bleed from the mouth. When the round ended, Jeffries was spitting blood and his seconds seemed tense and worried. *Paul Elcano Collection*

Round 14. Battered and bloody, Jeffries is led to his corner as the round ends. During the intermission only water was used in Johnson's corner and towels to fan him with. In Jeffries' corner they used everything they had.

Paul Elcano Collection

Round 15. Jeffries went down for the first time in his ring career after Johnson shot a left from his hip squarely into Jeffries' face, followed by a flurry of lefts and rights. Jeffries is seen here rising on the count of nine. *Paul Elcano Collection*

The Second KNOCKDOWN.

DANA
PHOTO. S.

Nº 101.

Round 15. Johnson knocked Jeffries to the canvas a second time with a left to the face. Jeffries fell through the ropes (not shown here) and several of his seconds got him back into the ring. He rose slowly to his feet on the count of nine. *Paul Elcano Collection*

Round 15. The third and final knockdown, after Johnson sent Jeffries reeling with a right to the head and a left to the nose. Between the count of seven and eight, Jeffries' seconds entered the ring, and this transgression of the rules ended the fight. *Paul Elcano Collection*

Jack Johnson is declared the winner of "The Fight of the Century." Tex Rickard in center of ring, flanked by Johnson and Jeffries. *Paul Elcano Collection*

"The Knockout" – as this photo is captioned by Dana – happened in the 15th round, after Jeffries had been knocked down twice before in the same round. Tex Rickard is shown at left. Moments after this photo was taken Jeffries' seconds entered the ring, ending the fight. *Paul Elcano Collection*

Original ink sketch of James Jeffries drawn by *San Francisco Examiner* sports journalist and cartoonist, Tad, in the autograph album of Frank Golden, Jr., July 6, 1910. *Nevada Historical Society*

Street scene outside Hotel Golden as Jack Johnson collected his share of the $100,000 purse the evening of July 4, 1910. *Courtesy*

Le Petit Journal

ADMINISTRATION
61, RUE LAFAYETTE, 61

Les manuscrits ne sont pas rendus

On s'abonne sans frais
dans tous les bureaux de poste

5 CENT.

SUPPLÉMENT ILLUSTRÉ

5 CENT.

ABONNEMENTS

21 me Année

Numéro 1.026

SEINE et SEINE-ET-OISE... 2 fr.   3 fr. 50
DÉPARTEMENTS............ 2 fr.   4 fr.
ÉTRANGER .... 2 50   5 fr.

DIMANCHE 17 JUILLET 1910

LA VICTOIRE DU NÈGRE

Jack Johnson met Jim Jeffries « knock-out » au championnat de boxe du monde

The fight attracted attention all over the world. In Paris, *Le Petit Journal* featured the fight on the front cover in full color. The artist was not present at the fight, but nevertheless included some imaginative details. Note in front the Chinaman at left, the cowboy in center, and a man in formal dress at right, and hats tossed into the ring. *Author's collection*

Johnson in the driver's seat of one of his racing cars, Doc Furey beside him. Furey had been one of Johnson's cornermen in the fight in Reno, July 4, 1910. Johnson fancied himself as good a racing driver as any professional and challenged Barney Oldfield to a race. Johnson lost. He qualified as a racing driver and was granted a license by the Contest Board. Later, he announced he planned to enter the Indianapolis 500 and the Hawthorne Park Meet in 1911. The American Automobile Association threatened to cancel both events if he did. *Library of Congress*

"Fireman" Jim Flynn arriving in Las Vegas, New Mexico for his fight with Jack Johnson. *Michael Holland Collection*

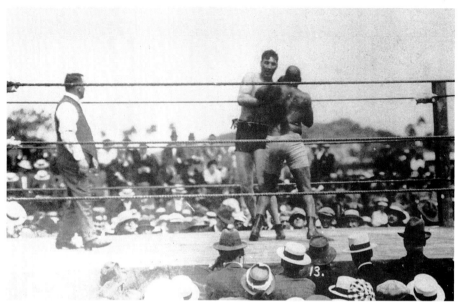

The Jack Johnson – Jess Willard championship fight was held in Havana, Cuba, April 5, 1915, and lasted 26 rounds. Willard was 6 feet 6 inches tall and weighed 250 pounds, and in this photograph Johnson looks small in comparison. *Author's collection*

A panorama of the ring and arena at the Oriental Park Race Track at Havana, Cuba. Sixteen thousand people attended the fight. Note the motion picture camera at bottom center. Rights to the film were in dispute after the fight and Johnson realized only a pittance from them. After the Havana fight, Johnson never again got a shot at the title. Willard lost the title to Jack Dempsey on July 4, 1919. *Author's collection*

James Jeffries (right) and Frank Gotch, December 2, 1910. *Rick Reviglio Collection*

Jack Johnson appeared fit and fashionably dressed in t[...] photograph taken in 1922, several months after his [...] lease from Leavenworth federal prison. With him is B[...] Delaney, who worked as one of Johnson's trainers at t[...] Johnson-Jeffries fight in Reno in 1910. *Library of Congr[...]*

Johnson to Las Vegas and stayed with him in rented quarters. Curley arranged considerable publicity to attract a large gate, but the hoopla failed, and less than five thousand sports showed up for the fight. The gate was poorly managed and many got in free to watch the fight. Flynn was no match for Johnson. By the ninth round, Flynn was beaten and helpless, and police entered the ring and stopped the fight. Johnson was disappointed with the purse, less than what he might have earned from a short vaudeville tour.

Johnson had been looking for a business in which to invest some of his money, and when he returned to Chicago he was offered a proposition that not only appealed to his purse but his vanity as well. A Chicago brewery offered to put up most of the money to open a fashionable cabaret, where Johnson would be the host and nominal owner. It was called "Café de Champion," located just outside of the Levee district. According to Johnson, the cabaret gained considerable distinction among Chicago's elite because of its elegant décor. "In the furnishing and decoration of the cabaret, I had spared no expense nor effort… I had gained a comprehensive idea of decorative effects… I had also collected many fine works of art, curios, and novelties. These I used in providing the attractive features for which my cabaret gained considerable distinction. I displayed a few real Rembrandts which I had obtained in Europe… These were only a few of the art subjects which adorned the walls of the Cabaret de Champion."[9] The bar had been carved from polished mahogany, the floors were deeply carpeted, and the spittoons were made of silver with gold trim. Hanging alongside the alleged Rembrandts were large posters and photographs of Jack Johnson. On the second floor of the cabaret were two private dining rooms and a lavishly furnished apartment, occupied by Johnson and Etta, now married. On the evening of September 11, 1912, while Johnson was absent, the festive atmosphere of the cabaret was shattered by the sound of a pistol shot. Etta had shot herself in the head.

She had been despondent for days, had complained of severe headaches, and had cancelled a vacation trip that very afternoon. When Johnson returned, he saw a police car in front of the cabaret and a crowd milling around the entrance. Etta had been taken to Providence Hospital, where she died the next morning. Her suicide received sensational treatment by the press, which reflected poorly upon Johnson, not to mention the Café de Champion.

Some two months later there was another incident at the cabaret when shots were reported fired at Johnson by Adah Banks, a black entertainer at the club. Adah was jealous of Johnson's attention to any female other than herself, and she claimed to have shot him in the foot, but there is nothing to suggest Johnson was wounded at all. The alleged shooting made headlines in the Chicago newspapers and were copied elsewhere, leading the public to believe the Café de Champion was a den of iniquity. Adah was jealous of a newcomer to the club, Lucille Cameron, a white woman eighteen years of age. Lucille was a buxom woman with dark hair, rosy cheeks, and sparkling eyes, of the type often pictured in a Renoir painting. She had arrived in Chicago from Minneapolis in the spring of 1912 and was not the innocent she appeared to be. She had worked in Minneapolis as a prostitute before coming to Chicago.[10] She had come to Chicago of her own free will, much as young women and men always have been drawn to life in the big city. Lucille had some training in bookkeeping and secretarial work, and Johnson hired her to take care of his correspondence and manage the books at the cabaret. They were often seen together, in and out of the cabaret, and gossip had it they were a couple. Their relationship, coming so soon after Etta's suicide, and because Lucille was so young and fair and Johnson black and older, outraged many whites who saw Johnson as a kind of Svengali with hypnotic powers over young white women. There now appeared on the scene Lucille's mother from Minneapolis, Mrs. F. Cameron-Falconet, who must have known something of her daughter's indelicate past, but nevertheless portrayed her to the press as pure and virginal as the driven snow. She was as properly outraged as a mother hen protecting her chick. With her was a Chicago lawyer she had hired, who said he would have Johnson in jail in short order. In a confrontation at the Café de Champion, Lucille refused to leave with her mother. Johnson was polite with her, but when her lawyer made threats, Johnson asked them to leave the premises.

Mrs. F. Cameron-Falconet promptly pressed charges through her lawyer, accusing Johnson of abducting her daughter, and federal authorities arrested Johnson. Lucille was also taken into custody by agents of the Bureau of Investigation, the forerunner of the Federal Bureau of Investigation. Johnson was not particularly disturbed by these events. He believed the matter would be settled by the usual fine and admonition. And he was released on bail after putting up a cash bond. But Johnson had underestimated the gravity of the situation. The federal government had decided Jack Johnson was an undesirable, a blot upon the American character, and had begun building its case against him. Where Jeffries the "white hope" had failed, and with no suitable white hopes in the ranks of boxing to challenge Johnson, the federal government now picked up the totem of "white hope," and prepared to dispatch Johnson not in the ring but in the federal court system. It marshalled a force against Johnson that he could not hope to match: at least a dozen agents from the Bureau were set to work to gather evidence against him, and six attorneys from the Justice Department to put together a case so impressive it would send him to a federal prison. Agents confined Lucille to a hotel room in Chicago with armed guards watching the corridors. Ostensibly this was to keep her away from Johnson's hypnotic influence, but it violated her constitutional rights, and her bail was set at $25,000 – an outrageous sum when one considers she had broken no laws. Johnson raised the sum and offered it as bail, but the judge, Kennesaw Mountain Landis, refused it, ruling that Johnson was not a fit person to put up bail for Lucille. Mountain Landis was later appointed Baseball Commissioner, and during his tenure black athletes were routinely excluded from playing major league baseball.

While Lucille was being held incommunicado, social reformers staged a massive street demonstration which was more a show of force than a demonstration. The anti-vice parade was the joint effort of more than forty thousand people representing every reform group in Cook County. The grand marshal of the parade was Virginia Brooks, who sometimes carried a shotgun to dramatize her persona as a militant social crusader. The parade was spearheaded by a contingent of mounted police. Marchers carried large banners depicting the evils of saloons, race tracks, poolrooms, tobacco, prostitution, gambling, and other assorted social ills. The parade marked the beginning of a reform movement in Chicago that would sweep through the Levee district and dominate newspaper headlines for months, even years. A number of complaints poured into the Chicago City Council, probably orchestrated by the Anti-Vice League, urging them to close down the Café de Champion. When the resolution was read before a packed audience, the crowd cheered, the council voted, and the cabaret was history. The brewery that had backed Johnson withdrew its support and the Café de Champion closed its doors forever.

Meanwhile, Johnson's attorney's tried without success to free Lucille on a writ of habeas corpus. Not only was Johnson forbidden to see Lucille, but Johnson's attorney was also denied the right to see her. Mrs. Phillips Aldrich, of the Law and Order League, however, found it easy to visit Lucille. She had been brought in by the authorities to make Lucille see the error of her ways, but in particular to get Lucille to incriminate Johnson by stating he had bodily abducted her from Minneapolis. Johnson, of course, had done no such thing. He had never set eyes on Lucille Cameron until she was introduced to him one night in the cabaret, to which she had come of her own free will. Mrs. Aldrich spent some two hours trying to extract a "confession" from Lucille, but to no avail. On October 12, 1912, Lucille was brought before a federal grand jury and questioned at length, especially on the legal points of abduction, which involved the crossing of state lines, and whether her alleged abduction had involved force. So convinced were members of the grand jury and the Bureau of Investigation that Johnson had abducted Lucille from Minneapolis it never occurred to them he might actually be innocent of such charges. They were convinced he had, and their only concern was to collect evidence to support a conviction under the Mann Act. But Lucille had said nothing that could be used to build a case against Johnson. She said repeatedly she had come to Chicago of her own volition. Moreover, federal agents and the grand jury had come to believe Johnson was the boss of a white slavery ring, that he hired procurers to scout several states for white girls which he used for his own amusement and then, when he tired of them, forced into brothels. When questioned about this, Lucille said it was ridiculous. She was regarded by federal agents as an uncooperative if not hostile witness and whisked away, this time not to a hotel room, but to jail in Rockford, Illinois.

The Mann Act, or White Slavery Act as it was often called, was passed into law by Congress in 1910. It was one of the first pieces of legislation that gave the federal government jurisdiction and authority over the sexual conduct of private citizens. It was sponsored by James Robert Mann, a Republican congressman from Illinois, who believed the morals of the nation were at risk because of widespread white slavery. In particular, it made it a crime to transport women across state lines "for the purpose of prostitution or debauchery, or any other immoral purpose." The law cast a very wide net, was so broadly written that arbitrary interpretations could

be made since it included both voluntary and commercial consider-
ations. Any man traveling with a woman across a state line and
having sex with her, whether by consent or for pay, would be in violation of the Mann Act. Like Prohibition, it was another triumph
for social reformers who believed the best way to purify the
American character was to legislate morality. Critics of the Mann
Act said such matters were more properly a matter of civil law, and
no concern of the federal government. As the law was working its
way through Congress, a grand jury in New York City, whose fore-
man was John D. Rockerfeller Jr., issued a special report on commercial vice and white slavery, which it had been investigating for
six months. The investigation had found no evidence of organized
white slavery in New York City. But the report had no effect. Many
people across the nation were convinced white slavery was an issue
of enormous importance, probably because the subject was in itself
a sensational one, and wide open to exaggeration. For over-zealous
prosecutors and puritanical bureaucrats the Mann Act was a license
to spy on the private lives of American citizens, and sometimes to
send them to prison on questionable evidence. One of the innocent
victims of the Mann Act some years after its passage into law was
America's greatest architect, Frank Lloyd Wright, who was arrested
by federal agents in Minneapolis and put in jail for two days until he
could prove his innocence.[11] Unlike Prohibition, the Mann Act has
never been repealed. It remains federal law even today.

Jack Johnson, out on bail, whatever his other vices may have
been, was now perceived as a wicked and villainous black-white
slaver, a perception orchestrated by a hostile press and abetted by
federal agents. Lucille was the innocent he had corrupted, though
she had told the grand jury she had worked sometimes as a prostitute in Chicago three months before she met Johnson. She was kept
in jail in Rockford for weeks, though federal agents had come to realize she was of no value to them as a witness against Johnson. She

was probably kept in jail for two reasons: the first was to keep up the illusion before the public that she was a viable witness and had to be kept out of Johnson's reach, and second, that while in jail she might begin to despair of her confinement and cooperate with the authorities.

When agents realized they could not make a case against Johnson with Lucille as a witness, they began to explore other avenues. They hired informers who could keep them posted on Johnson's activities. They paid at least two, one of whom was a neighbor of Johnson's, who was asked to keep watch on the Johnson house and make reports of all comings and goings. Meanwhile, federal agents were working to trace prostitutes with whom Johnson had had sexual relations over the years. Most of these efforts failed to produce any evidence that could be used to build a case within the framework of the Mann Act. Finally, agents hit the jackpot when they located Belle Schreiber, almost under their very noses. She was working in a brothel in Washington, D.C. at 1229 D Street.[12] Belle had been out of the limelight ever since she had separated from Johnson in 1910, and she was only too willing to cooperate. Belle had a vindictive streak in her and she had not forgiven Johnson for choosing Etta Duryea over her. She would give agents all the information they needed to send Johnson to federal prison. As the detailed story of her life with Johnson unfolded, in which she gave dates and places, a slight problem developed. It was not her memory, for she was fairly accurate on details. Rather it was that nearly all of her association with Johnson had taken place before June, 1910, *before* the Mann Act was passed into law by Congress. There was, however, the trip she had made from Chicago to Reno in July, 1910, to attend the Johnson-Jeffries fight, a trip which she made alone. But there was another trip she made to see Johnson, from Pittsburgh to Chicago, on August 10, 1910. That particular trip, federal attorneys decided, would be enough to charge Johnson with transporting a woman across state lines for the purpose of prostitution and debauchery. Whether Belle had made the trip alone or in company with Johnson would not prove an obstacle, as the Mann Act, with its arbitrary language, could be bent a bit, if necessary, to accommodate the charge. But the Mann Act was rather specific on another point, one in Johnson's favor. It did not consider criminal a relationship of long standing and pre-existing immorality, such as that of a kept mistress and a man who might cross interstate lines. If this seems odd, it is because the trip might be considered to have other purposes in mind other than immoral ones. In any case, this fairly well describes the relationship between Belle and Johnson. This interpretation might have excused the behavior of a banker or a politician traveling with his mistress, and the case probably would have been dropped. But Johnson was neither a banker nor a politician, and the loophole in the law was not designed for persons of his station. The public was crying for Johnson's scalp. Federal attorneys had decided Belle would make a good witness, make a favorable impression upon a jury, and with careful handling by the prosecution even gain sympathy from the court. She was booked into a hotel room in Washington, D.C., and each day agents encouraged her to remember everything she could.

Belle was brought secretly to Chicago to testify before the grand jury. After hours of testimony, the grand jury handed down the indictment, which was sent on to Judge Mountain Landis in a sealed envelope. He promptly issued a bench warrant for Johnson's arrest and Johnson was again taken into custody. Belle was rushed from the courthouse to the railroad station, where she was escorted by agents back to Washington, D.C. Meanwhile, Lucille remained in jail at Rockford, though federal attorneys no longer had any use for her as a witness. When Johnson was arrested again, his attorney appeared before Mountain Landis and requested bail. Landis replied: "I will not accept a cash bond in this case. There is a human cry in this case that cannot be overlooked in consideration of a bond."[13]

Lucille had proved an embarrassment to the government. The public had been led to believe – because of statements given to the press by her mother, Mrs. F. Cameron-Falconet – that Lucille would be the star witness in the government's case. When Lucille refused to cooperate, that prospect vanished. Then, as though to confound matters further, a new witness suddenly appeared, a mystery woman who suddenly appeared and disappeared under armed escort, Belle Schreiber, who would give evidence necessary to convict Johnson. Perhaps Judge Landis realized that were Lucille to be released from jail she would promptly return to Johnson, and that might prove a further embarrassment. The fact that Lucille had been kept in jail for many weeks in violation of her constitutional rights did not seem to disturb Judge Landis. But finally, late in November, Lucille was quietly released. She stayed with her mother in a Chicago hotel for one day, then slipped away.

After much haggling before Judge Landis, bail was finally granted Johnson, after he had spent more than a week in jail. Lucille did precisely what her mother and the government feared: she went directly to Johnson's house. A few days later they were married in a private ceremony. When Mrs. F. Cameron-Falconet learned her daughter had married Jack Johnson, she seemingly had a fit of apoplexy and had to be treated for shock. Many observers said Johnson had married Lucille because a wife is not required to testify against her husband, that it was simply a marriage based on expediency. But if such were the case, it would seem that Johnson would have married Belle rather than Lucille, as Lucille no longer figured in the government's case. In any event, the marriage stirred up more resentment against Johnson. Etta had been dead and buried only three months, and he had married another white woman. One Congressman shouted: "In Chicago, white girls are made the slaves of an African brute."[14] Federal agents, meanwhile, were preparing the indictment based on Belle's testimony. It listed eleven violations of the Mann Act, including prostitution, debauchery, unlawful sexual intercourse, and crimes against nature.

The trial was scheduled for May, 1913, which gave Johnson's attorneys six months to prepare for trial. The reason for the delay was because Judge George Carpenter, who would hear the case, had doubts about the constitutionality of the Mann Act, and did not want to go to trial before the Supreme Court had ruled on its legality. Johnson's lawyers felt the specific charges of the indictment could be countered by Johnson's testimony; after all, his word was as good as Belle's. But on the matter of transporting Belle across state lines they were not so confident. Their line of defense on that question – the constitutionality of the Mann Act – would by then have been decided by the Supreme Court.

The delay in scheduling the trial posed somewhat of a problem for the government. What to do with Belle for six long months? What she wanted to do, she told federal agents, was to go back to her way of life, drinking and whoring at the brothel in Washington, D.C. Obviously that would not do. It might damage her credibility as a witness. Johnson's biographer, Randy Roberts, who gained access to the government's file on Jack Johnson in the National Archives, which contains field reports of Bureau of Investigation agents,[15] discovered that Belle was kept in several places during this interval: New York City, Washington, D.C., and Baltimore. Belle was not at all happy about being kept on a leash; her behavior was often cantankerous and perverse. To keep her in a good mood, federal agents were assigned to take her out to dinner – sometimes every night – to buy her liquor, take her out to the theater and cinema, and otherwise keep her amused. If she was not catered to and pampered, she grew testy and unpleasant. Finally, in early May, Belle and her escorts boarded a train for Chicago, where, on the witness stand, she would have her moment in the limelight.

She made a good witness, giving dates, places, and describing her travels in detail. She had had six months in which to polish her testimony, and she had probably been coached. Johnson's attorneys made many objections, but few were allowed. The jury of twelve white men listened attentively. At one point Belle complained: "I was driven out of disreputable houses [brothels] in Pittsburgh, Cleveland, and other cities. They didn't want me because I was Jack Johnson's white sweetheart. Bad as the places were, I was too bad to remain in them."[16] Asked if she ever loved Johnson, Belle answered: "I don't believe I did. I don't believe I ever knew what love was."[17] Federal attorneys called a number of witnesses to confirm Belle's testimony, but much of it was in the realm of hearsay evidence.

Johnson's attorneys raised objections that the prosecution had failed to introduce physical evidence to support the testimony of its witnesses, such as railroad tickets, hotel receipts, baggage claim tickets, letters, telegrams, etc., but were generally overruled. Johnson was not passive when he took the witness stand in his own defense, nor was he arrogant. On cross-examination he was straightforward and emphatic in reply to questions federal attorney's put to him. He matched wits with them, and when questions were re-phrased in such a way as to catch him in a contradiction of what he had previously said, he recognized the trick and neatly sidestepped. If a prosecutor asked him leading questions, he knew the strategy and refused to be trapped. While on the stand he volunteered very little, sticking to a simple yes or no whenever possible. He was never contrite, as befits one who assumes the role of scapegoat. He made no apologies for his lifestyle. He refused to bend and genuflect before his accusers.

In summing up, Johnson's attorney told the jury the Mann Act was poor legislation (by now it had been favorably ruled upon by the Supreme Court), but even as written, there was no hard evidence to suggest Johnson had violated it. The federal prosecutor, in turn, sought to play upon the emotions of the jury when he said: "If you should find the defendant not guilty, knowing as you do the evidence in this case, I do not see how you could ever look squarely in the faces of those persons whom you respect and admire, and especially how you could ever look squarely into the faces of your mothers, wives, and daughters." [18]

If the government's case against Johnson was not impressive on the face of the evidence presented, it was impressive in bulk and size, supported by a small bureaucracy and a mountain of paperwork. The jury was out less than two hours. On the fourth ballot the jury agreed Johnson was guilty on four of the eleven counts in the indictment. The counts dropped had to do with crimes against nature and debauchery. The remaining four had to do with transporting Belle from Pittsburgh to Chicago, and in the minds of the jurors' Johnson's intentions had been for sexual purposes, if not white slavery. After the verdict was read, one of the federal attorneys said for publication: "This verdict... is the forerunner of laws to be passed in these United States which we may live to see – laws forbidding miscegenation. This Negro, in the eyes of many, has been persecuted. Perhaps as an individual he was. But it was his misfortune to be the foremost example of the evil in permitting the intermarriage of whites and blacks." [19] Later, during the sentencing phase of the trial, Judge Carpenter touched on the same theme when he said: "We have had a number of defendants found guilty in this court of violations of the Mann Act who have been sentenced to severe punishment, from one to two years in the penitentiary. This defendant is one of the best known men of his race, and his example has been far-reaching, and the court is bound to consider the position he occupied among his people. In view of these facts, this is a case that calls for more than a fine." [20] Inferred in both these statements is the notion that should an individual because of his achievement rise above the commonplace he therefore risks being singled out for special punishment. Jack Johnson, according to such thinking, had to be made an example of. Moreover, these statements seem to excuse government persecution of an individual citizen, as though to say if the government had not convicted Johnson under the Mann Act it would have been perfectly proper to do so under some other pretext.

Johnson had never wanted to be a symbol or an icon. All he wanted was the title of world's heavyweight champion. But the trial and the publicity it generated had transfigured him into a symbol of the "bad nigger" – and made of him a national scapegoat. On June 4, 1913, he was sentenced to one year in a federal prison and a fine of $1,000. He was given two weeks to file an appeal. He still held the title. But a year in a federal prison could cost him a quarter of a million dollars in lost purses and vaudeville contracts. He had two weeks to make a decision: either go to prison, or jump bail and leave the United States. Oddly, federal agents believed it would be best if Johnson left the country: "I believe we all agree… on the advantage to the country if Johnson were to be exiled from it," one federal agent wrote to his superior in the Bureau of Investigation.[21]

Accompanied by his wife Lucille, his two favorite racing cars and a mountain of baggage, Johnson arrived in Hamilton, Ontario a week later, skipping bail. How he managed to elude the watchful eyes of informers and federal agents is not altogether clear. In his autobiography, Johnson told how he switched places with a black baseball player whose team was enroute to Canada for an exhibition game. This version has gained wide acceptance, but it is probably more folklore that Johnson invented for his autobiography. Months later, when Johnson was in Paris, he gave an interview to a reporter from the *Chicago Examiner*,[22] giving another version of how he had managed to elude federal agents. He said he had bribed two of them for $50,000 in cash. Going further, he said he had also bribed the

District Attorney's office in Cook County, and then named the two bag men who had delivered the cash. The allegation was serious enough – supported by members of Johnson's family – to convene a grand jury investigation into the matter. But it was a cursory affair and the accused agents were not indicted.

Some considerable planning was required on Johnson's part to book tickets, make arrangements for the shipping of his cars and possessions, and other details. Johnson, his wife Lucille, and his nephew, Gus Rhodes, made their way from Hamilton to Montreal, where they boarded the liner *Corinthian* on June 29, 1913, and sailed for Europe. And so began seven years of exile.

His travels abroad took him to England, France, Russia, Belgium, Spain, Argentina, Mexico and Cuba. In England, he had hoped for fights that would replenish his depleted bank account, but his old adversary there, the National Sporting Club, offered him only one fight with a ridiculously cheap purse, and he refused it. He fared better on the English vaudeville circuit until the novelty of his performance wore thin. In France he fought two bouts, one with Jim Johnson, the other with Frank Moran. He made very little from these fights. In the fight with Moran the purse was tied up in litigation for the remainder of his lifetime. In Russia he toured in the grand style. It was the twilight of the Romanov dynasty, and World War I was looming on the horizon. He met Rasputin, whom he described as big as Jim Jeffries, dressed in a monk's robe, who drank wine sloppily and radiated a foul body odor. Johnson's patron in Russia was a wealthy black man – either English or American – known as George Thomas. Thomas claimed to be on intimate terms with the Imperial Court, and said he had access to the Czar himself. Before Johnson left Russia, he said Thomas came to him one night and handed him a packet of letters bearing the Imperial seal, told him never to let them out of his sight, to guard them with his life, and take them to London. Under no circumstances must the letters be allowed to fall into the hands of the Germans. "What are they?" asked Johnson. "Copies of private messages between the Czar and the Kaiser," Thomas answered. Whether there is any truth to this story is a matter of speculation. But as rumors of war swept across Europe, and as Johnson traveled from one country to another (whether he actually carried secret documents or not) the federal government back in Washington began to take an interest in his movements.

Before he left Paris, Johnson out of necessity did a few wrestling matches, a humiliation to any champion boxer. (Some forty years later, Joe Louis, who needed the money, would also enter the wrestling ring.) Johnson then traveled to Spain, where he was unable to find a suitable boxing match. He became friends with Joselito and Belmonte, two of the greatest bullfighters of the day. Both encouraged him to enter the bullring, but not until they had given him careful lessons in the art of the cape and the sword. After weeks of instruction, Johnson was ready. His debut was at the ring in Barcelona, and a huge crowd had gathered to see the world's heavyweight champion fight a bull. Joselito and Belmonte were on hand to give him encouragement, and Belmonte even insisted that Johnson use his personal scarlet cape. The President of Spain paid Johnson a visit before the fight and wished him well. In the ring, Johnson worked his bull with the cape expertly, arcing the cape with the sweeping flourishes Joselito had taught him. He was as quick in the bullring as he was in the boxing ring, sidestepping the charges of the bull, judging the distance between himself and the horns with uncanny accuracy. But when it came to the sword, driving it between the bull's horns, he was not so good. He missed twice, but on the third try he found his mark, and the bull fell at his feet. The crowd roared, and Belmonte led Johnson to a spot before the Presidential box where he was showered with roses. But once in the bullring was enough. He preferred the relative safety of the wrestling ring, where he defeated the Castelian champion in Barcelona, and the national champion, Juan Ochoa, in Bilbao.

With World War I raging across Europe, public interest was focused on the battlefronts, casualties, and air-raids. It would have been next to impossible to arrange for a boxing match in most continental cities. The Germans were lobbing shells into Paris from a distance of sixty miles with their famous Paris railroad gun. London was bombed by zeppelins. Johnson did return to London for a vaudeville tour, but it was not as successful as his first. Rather than return to Spain, he sailed for Argentina. On December 15, 1914, he fought Jack Murray in Buenos Aires and won with a knockout in the third round.

It had been four years since Johnson had fought Jeffries in Reno. In those four years he had not fought a top-ranked contender. He trained infrequently, and when he did train for the few fights he had during these years he did not work hard, believing he could win easily over his lesser opponents. He was now thirty-six years old, at an age when a heavyweight boxer is usually past his prime. Years of easy living – plus his appetite for good food and champagne – has softened him. But he was still the most skillful boxer in the ring.

In 1916, Jack Curley, a fight promoter, told Johnson he could arrange a title fight with Jess Willard, the new "white hope," but that the fight would have to be held somewhere in Mexico. Johnson was interested. He left it to Curley to work out the details with Mexican politicians, who at the time exercised control over various parts of the country. In the north, Pancho Villa was in charge. In the south, Zapata. President Venustiano Carranza controlled the central portion and most of the seaports. Curley had wanted the fight held in Juarez, across the river from El Paso, Texas. Pancho Villa was agreeable. But for Johnson to reach Juarez (he could not travel in the United States) he would have to travel through Carranza country and be given safe conduct. Carranza said this could be arranged if he were given a large share of the purse, otherwise Johnson would be arrested. Curley said he would think it over.

Meanwhile, Johnson was in Havana, engaged in a vaudeville tour. When Curley met Johnson there to tell him about the problems in arranging the fight in Mexico, Johnson said, "Why not here, in Havana?" Curley said he would look into it. He met with President Mario Menocal, who told Curley the fight would be welcome in Cuba as long as there was no scandal attached to it. Word went out to the news services around the world that the fight would be held at the Oriental Park Race Track in Havana, April 5, 1915.

Jess Willard was called by the sporting press "The Pottawatomie Giant," the word Pottawatomie coming from the county in western Kansas where Willard had been born. He stood six feet six inches tall and weighed two hundred and fifty pounds. Starting out as a rank amateur, his early fights were undistinguished. His only asset was a powerful punch – if and when it landed. But by 1914, he had improved, pushed into a rigorous training program by his new manager, Tom Jones, a retired Chicago barber. When Willard arrived at his training camp in Havana, he was in excellent condition, and he trained hard each day – even in bad weather – to prepare for the fight. Perhaps he had heard that Johnson had grown soft after years of easy living and was vulnerable.

Johnson probably regarded Willard as an easy opponent, despite his great size. Willard wasn't in the same league as Luther McCarthy, Jim Flynn or Bombardier Wells. Johnson was lax in his training. When he should have done eight miles of roadwork, he would quit at four. He worked out with his sparring partners in much the same way as Jeffries had in Reno back in 1910 – infrequently and indifferently. When he should have been training, he could be seen driving his racing car along one of Havana's sandy beaches. He had wired friends in Chicago he would put Willard away in the fifteenth round, and backed it up by betting $2,500 on himself to win.

On the day of the fight some sixteen thousand people filled the arena. The day was hot and still. Willard entered the ring wearing a ten-gallon cowboy hat. When he took off his robe he revealed an impressive body hardened by months of training. Johnson looked small by comparison; his stomach was not as hard and flat as Willard's. But he took the fight to Willard at once, landing a succession of punches. Willard moved awkwardly, often flat-footed, his long left arm extended, jabbing to little effect. At the end of the first ten rounds Johnson was ahead on points.

The heat seemed to cause Johnson some problems. He perspired heavily. But he had saved something for the upcoming rounds. In the twelfth he increased the pace, landing lefts and rights to Willard's face and ribs. He drove Willard into corners and pounded him relentlessly. In the fifteenth, he thought Willard was ready for the knockout and he hit him with everything he had, but he could not knock him out. Willard survived the fifteenth and though battered and cut was still on his feet. But Johnson was now visibly tired. His blows no longer had the power to knock Willard out. For a few more rounds he tried and did land several hard blows, but Willard would not go down. They had now fought for over an hour, and Johnson realized he could not last the full forty-five rounds. The crowd sensed Johnson was slowing down, weakening. Willard seemed to gain a second wind but was not quite sure how to press his advantage against Johnson. When Johnson went to his corner at the end of the twenty-fifth round, he told Jack Curley to take Lucille out of the arena, that he could not last much longer. He came out slowly for the twenty-sixth. Willard sensed the moment was at hand. He hit Johnson on the face and chest, then with a haymaker that landed squarely on Johnson's chin. He fell to the canvas. The referee started to count. Johnson lay on his back, his elbows bent so that it seemed his gloves shaded his eyes from the sun. Then his arms fell to the canvas, and he was counted out. The photograph of the knockdown, taken by photographer Fred Mace of New York City, would become one of the most famous in all boxing history, argued over for years to come. For those who believed Johnson had thrown the fight, the photograph was all the proof they needed, which seemingly showed Johnson shading his eyes from the sun with his gloves while the referee counted him out. What they overlooked was that a moment later his arms fell to the canvas and he lay there for the rest of the count.

As soon as the fight was over, Johnson said to reporters that the best man had won. Nothing was said about throwing the fight. But a year later, in 1916, he said he had allowed Willard to win, and in his autobiography he repeats it in more detail. Curiously – and there is a similarity here – Jeffries said immediately after the fight with Johnson in Reno in 1910 that the best man had won. Then he changed his mind and said he had lost because he had been doped before the fight, a story he elaborated upon in his autobiography. Johnson said he had been given assurances by Jack Curley and his associates that if he threw the fight the government would allow him to return to the United States without having to serve a prison sentence.[23] Of course, Curley was in no position to give such assurances. When Johnson had been in Chicago waiting trial in 1913, he had approached federal attorneys about bargaining and they had turned him down. Johnson should have known better, and this makes the story all the more suspect. If that were not enough, Johnson said the reason he waited for the twenty-sixth round was because he was to be paid the balance due him for the fall when all the money had been counted in the cashier's cage, in five-hundred dollar bills. There are two things wrong here. First, most of the money in the cashier's cage was probably in Cuban pesos, not American dollars. And second, bills of five-hundred dollar denomination were a rarity in Cuba, and it is most unlikely there would have been many in the cage at Oriental Park. Johnson's story – or rationalization – is no more valid than the story Jeffries told. Johnson's effort to knock Willard out in the fifteenth round spent most of his strength. The fight would never have lasted another eleven rounds had it not been for Johnson's defensive boxing ability. Nat Fleischer, Jack Curley, Jess Willard, and others agreed the fight was honest and that Johnson had been knocked out.

Johnson had hoped to return to the United States after the Willard fight. Perhaps the government would relent, now that he had lost his title. He wrote his lawyers in Chicago to put out a few inquiries. A reply came back promptly: he would surely be arrested and sent to prison if he returned. He felt he had been betrayed, if not by Curley and his associates, then by overzealous bureaucrats in Washington, D.C.

For the next few years, Johnson and Lucille wandered from England to Spain to Mexico. He had three fights in Spain, none of them with ranked contenders. One curious bout took place in Barcelona, with Arthur Craven, who had a reputation not as a boxer but as a painter and poet. Johnson won that one in a waltz. In 1919, he went to Mexico where he was welcomed by President Carranza. Carranza had his own reasons for befriending Johnson, which had to do with troubled political relations with Washington. President Woodrow Wilson's policies toward Mexico at the time were contradictory and patronizing. Carranza knew Johnson was a thorn in Washington's political hide, so he used the opportunity to court Johnson as an affront to the Yankee gringos. A match was arranged between Johnson and Tom Cowler of England. Cowler had fought some big names earlier in his career, but like Johnson was now past his prime. Nevertheless, the bout in Mexico City drew a huge gate, and Carranza sat in the Presidential box. The fight lasted for twelve rounds and Johnson won by a knockout. He had five more fights in Mexico, one of them in Tia Juana on May 17, 1920, when he fought George Roberts, and won by a knockout in the third round. Then President Carranza was assassinated while fleeing the country and a new revolutionary government came to power. Those who had been friendly with Carranza and enjoyed his patronage were rounded up and shot. Johnson escaped such a fate because he was not a Mexican national, but there was talk of arresting him and turning him over to the American authorities. His boxing permits and licenses were revoked, and suddenly he found himself without any means of earning a living. He was, in effect, *persona non grata*, and the next move by the revolutionary government might be to deport him. Both he and Lucille were ambivalent about returning home, but friends in California and Chicago advised him it would be best to return. He and Lucille could not live the rest of their lives in exile.

On July 20, 1920, Johnson crossed the border near Tia Juana and turned himself in. His surrender to federal authorities made newspaper headlines across the nation. The mood of the country had changed during his years abroad. The war was over. There was a feeling of euphoria in the air, people were a bit more tolerant. America was on the threshold of the Jazz Age. Many were inclined to forgive him; others saw him as a kind of anti-Establishment hero. As his train made its way toward Chicago, people turned out for a glimpse of him. He was accompanied by federal agents, but he was not handcuffed. As always, he was impeccably dressed in a tailored suit, polished patent leather shoes, carrying his gold-topped cane. Several thousand blacks had gathered at the Chicago railroad station to greet him. But federal authorities, who wanted no such demonstration in his honor, had the train stopped at Geneva, on the outskirts of Chicago. Johnson was held in jail there, waiting an appearance before Judge George A. Carpenter. Much to the annoyance of federal agents, Johnson was treated like a celebrity in the

Geneva jail. He was allowed to order meals from restaurants, receive visitors, and on one occasion to take a ride in an automobile.
He appeared before Judge Carpenter on September 14, 1920.
During his exile, Johnson's lawyers had succeeded in an appeals
court in having some of the charges dismissed, but not his pur-
ported violation of the Mann Act. His lawyers argued for leniency
but Judge Carpenter, who had sentenced Johnson seven years before, had not changed his mind. "I see no reason for making a
change in the sentence. If the conduct of the defendant had been
such as to indicate that he regretted his criminal act, I might feel
differently about a reduction of sentence. On the contrary, Johnson
has behaved in such a manner to indicate a complete disregard for
the laws and institutions of this country."[24] Carpenter handed down
his sentence. Johnson would serve one year in the federal penitentiary at Leavenworth, Kansas.

At Leavenworth prison, Johnson was surprised to meet an
old acquaintance, Denver S. Dickerson, who had been Governor of
Nevada when the Johnson-Jeffries fight was held in Reno, was now
the prison superintendent at Leavenworth. Dickerson told Johnson
that as long as he behaved himself he would have no trouble at
Leavenworth. He appointed Johnson athletic director of the prison
and allowed him to box as much as he pleased. Dickerson even
arranged three bouts for Johnson, all attended by large crowds at
the prison, and which were filmed. He fought George Owens and
won by a knockout in six rounds. On March 18, 1921, he fought
George Boykin and won by a knockout in five rounds, and finally he
met and defeated Jack Townsend in six rounds, winning by a knockout. Johnson trained almost every day, and when he was released on
July 9, 1921, he was in good spirits and fine condition. Although now
forty-two years old, he told reporters he was ready to take on Jack
Dempsey, who now held the title. But Dempsey had drawn the color
line and would not fight a black boxer, not even a former champion.

In Chicago, fans and admirers gave him a rousing homecoming celebration. Later, in Harlem, he was welcomed with all the enthusiasm of a hero returning from the wars – with a parade in his honor, Johnson himself as grand marshal, dressed in a checkered suit, waving his cane, flashing his golden smile at the cheering crowd.

Whatever dreams Johnson had for a comeback would not come true. The boxing game had changed a great deal during his exile. Power now rested in the hands of a few promoters and managers – a sort of exclusive club. His old friend Tex Rickard had left the boxing game and now owned a cattle ranch in South America larger than the state of Rhode Island. Black boxers were still confined to a league of their own, much as in baseball and other sports. Moreover, Johnson was in his early forties and most boxing professionals believed his career was over. It was not until February 20, 1923, that he got a fight, and not a very good one, with Homer Smith in Montreal. He won by a decision in ten rounds, but it was not the old Jack Johnson. One of his last fights was in Nogales, Mexico on May 5, 1926, when he fought Pat Lester. He was forty-eight years old. Lester was a strapping young heavyweight considered to be a contender against Dempsey for the title. In this fight Johnson proved he still had the skills of a great boxer, defeating Lester in fifteen rounds. In 1921, a few days before Christmas, Sam McVey died in a Harlem hospital. Johnson had fought him three times, and said of all the men he had met in the ring, McVey was the toughest. Along with Joe Jeanette and Sam Langford, McVey in his prime had been an excellent black boxer. He died broke and would have been buried in a pauper's grave had it not been for Johnson. Though he had little money at the time, Johnson raised enough to give McVey a decent burial and erect a headstone over his grave.

In 1924, Lucille Cameron filed for a divorce. It was granted without contest. She had remained with Johnson during his most turbulent years: his trial, his years of exile, his imprisonment, and the years immediately following his release, when he had little or no money. It is a tribute to this woman that she remained loyal to Johnson when government agents tried to persuade her to testify against him. After the divorce she refused to be interviewed by the press, she did not write a sensational biography, and lived in quiet seclusion the rest of her life.

After his boxing career was over, Johnson tried his hand at a number of things to earn a living. He promoted a few fights in Mexico, was a representative for a Canadian brewery, sold stocks and bonds, appeared as a minor player in grand opera, nightclub master of ceremonies, attraction at circuses and carnivals, and for a short time was even a bit player on the Warner Brothers lot in Hollywood. In his later years, he found somewhat steady employment at Hubert's Museum on West Forty-Second Street in New York City. There, among the fortune-tellers, arcade machines, memorabilia exhibits, and other miscellaneous attractions, Johnson would appear on a platform and entertain his audience with recollections of his great fights with Jeanette, McVey, Langford, Ketchel, Burns, Jeffries, and Willard. He took questions and comments from the audience and his lively repartee made him the most popular attraction at the museum.

In spite of his reduced circumstances, he always had a place to live, wore fashionable clothes, and owned a fast and expensive automobile. He still appeared regularly in traffic court, cited for a variety of moving violations. It was the old obsession with speed, the extension of power he felt at the wheel of an automobile – or the need to be moving fast, leaving everyone behind in his wake. And finally, on June 10, 1946, it proved his undoing. He was driving to New York City from Texas, where he had toured with a small Texas circus. Near Franklinton, North Carolina, driving fast, he lost control of his Lincoln Zephyr and crashed into a power pole. His companion in the car, Fred. L. Scott, was not seriously injured, but Johnson was. He was taken to a hospital in Raleigh, and died shortly after his arrival.

On June 14, at the Pilgrim Baptist Church in Chicago, thousands of blacks gathered for a final tribute to Jack Johnson. From the church the procession made its way to Graceland Cemetery where he was buried beside Etta Duryea Johnson. Of those who came that day to pay their last respects, few could have put into words why or how he had influenced their lives. During his years as champion, much nonsense had been written about "white hopes," which diminished the sense of the word *hope*. But without ever intending it, for Johnson was never a crusader for causes except his own, he inspired a sense of hope, in the true meaning of the word, to many people.

Some writers have said that Jack Johnson poisoned the well for would-be black athletes to follow, that it took decades until they were accepted into championship circles. But one must remember that in Johnson's time (and for years afterward) black athletes had not been accepted, except into leagues of their own, such as the black baseball leagues. Black athletes were not allowed to participate in white competition tennis, cycling, football, baseball, basketball and other sports. In some instances, commissioners appointed to oversee a particular sport felt it their duty to exclude blacks. It was a time of segregation, not only in sports, but in many social and economic aspects of American life. In spite of these obstacles, Johnson fought his way to the top and remained there for seven years. It was a remarkable achievement against overwhelming odds, and it helped to prepare the way, in years to come, for black athletes such as Jackie Robinson, Joe Louis, Jesse Owens, and many more. Johnson was the first black athlete to win an international title – world's heavyweight champion – the crown jewel of boxing. Arthur Ashe, Jr., the late tennis champion, paid him the highest tribute when he remarked that Jack Johnson, in his opinion, was the most significant black athlete in history.

NOTES

PRELIMINARIES

1. Johnson would fight Klondike again in 1901 and 1902, and win both fights. Johnson, Jack. *Jack Johnson – in the Ring – and Out. With introductory Articles by "TAD," Ed W. Smith, Damon Runyon, and Mrs. Jack Johnson.* Chicago: National Sports Publishing Company, 1927, p.257.
2. Fullerton, Hugh. *Two Fisted Jeff.* Chicago: Consolidated Book Publishers, [1929], p.vii.
3. Johnson, Jack, p.43.
4. Farr, Finis. *Black Champion: the Life and Times of Jack Johnson.* New York: Charles Scribner's Sons. 1964, p.24.
5. *Ibid.,* p.15.
6. *Johnson, Jack, p.44-46.*
7. *San Francisco Chronicle,* July 4, 1910.
8. Johnson, Jack, p.49.
9. *Ibid.,* p.50.
10. Batchelor, Denzil. *Jack Johnson and his Times.* London: Weidenfeld and Nicolson, 1990. pp.53-54.
11. Fullerton, Hugh, p.129.
12. *Ibid.,* p.135.
13. *Ibid.,* pp.241-242.
14. *Ibid.,* pp.243-244.
15. Johnson, Jack, p.53.
16. *Ibid.,* p.54.
17. Lynch, Bohun. *Knuckles and Gloves.* New York: Henry Holt & Co., 1923, p.151.

18. *Ibid.*, p.149.
19. Johnson, Jack, p.52.

The Fight at Rushcutter's Bay

1. Batchelor, Denzil, p.67.
2. Johnson, Jack, pp.163-164.
3. Roberts, Randy. *Papa Jack: Jack Johnson and the Era of White Hopes.* New York: Free Press, 1983, p.57.
4. *Ibid.*, p.58
5. Johnson, Jack, p.165.
6. Batchelor, Denzil, pp.68-69; Roberts, Randy, p.60.
7. Johnson, Jack, p.166.
8. Lynch, Bohun, p.152.
9. Johnson, Jack, pp.166-167.
10. *New York Herald*, Dec. 27, 1908.
11. Johnson, Jack, p.76.
12. Batchelor, Denzil, p.78.

Contradictions

1. Johnson, Jack, p.77.
2. *Ibid.*, p.73.
3. *Ibid.*, p.76.
4. Washburn, Charles. *Come into my Parlor. A Biography of the Aristocratic Everleigh Sisters of Chicago.* [New York, 1936.]
5. Johnson, Jack, p.78.
6. *Ibid.*, p.78.
7. *Ibid.*, p.76.
8. Lardner, John, *White Hopes and other Tigers.* Philadelphia: J. P. Lippincott, 1951., pp.34-35.
9. Johnson, Jack, p.232.
10. *New York Herald*, July 3, 1920, Magazine section, p.6, "The Wanderings of a Championship."
11. *Ibid.*, p.6.
12. *Ibid.*, p.6.
13. Johnson, Jack, p.169.
14. Lardner, John, p.36.
15. *San Francisco Examiner*, July 3, 1910, Jeffries, James, "The Story of my Life."

16. Fullerton, Hugh, p.244.
17. *Ibid.*, p.272.
18. *Ibid.*, p.273.
19. *Ibid.*, p.274.

THE LONG ROAD TO RENO

1. Fullerton, Hugh, p.275.
2. Samuels, Charles, *The Magnificent Rube; the Life and Times of Tex Rickard.* N.Y.: McGraw-Hill, 1957, pp.142-143.
3. For further discussion of the social reform movement in America during this period, see Farr, Finis, pp.150-155; also see Roberts, Randy, pp.93-96.
4. Roberts, Randy, pp.93-94.
5. *Ibid.*, p. 97.
6. Farr, Finis, p.82.
7. *Ibid.*, p.153.
8. Roberts, Randy, pp.97-98.
9. *Ibid.*, p.98.
10. Farr, Finis, p.81.
11. *Ibid.*, p.85.
12. *Ibid.*, p.86.
13. *Ibid.*, p.86.
14. Samuels, Charles, p.159.
15. Farr, Finis, p.89.
16. *Ibid.*, p.89.
17. *San Francisco Chronicle*, June 21, 1910.
18. *New York Herald*, June 24, 1910.
19. *San Francisco Chronicle*, June 20, 1910.
20. *Ibid.*
21. Samuels, Charles, p.159.
22. Fullerton, Hugh, pp.277-278.
23. *San Francisco Examiner*, June 21, 1910.
24. *Reno Gazette*, June 25, 1910.
25. *San Francisco Chronicle*, June 22, 1910.

"NEVADA, THE LAST FREE STATE"

1. *Nevada State Journal*, June 20, 1910.
2. *Reno Gazette*, June 21, 1910.
3. *Ibid.*, July 1, 1910.

4. *Nevada State Journal,* June 23, 1910.
5. *San Francisco Examiner,* June 29, 1910.
6. *Everybody's Magazine,* April, 1907, pp.464-474, Rex Beach, "The Fight at Tonopah."
7. Fleischer, Nat. *Jack Dempsey. The true story of the Manassa Mauler.* N.Y.: Bantam, 1949, p.72.
8. *Everybody's Magazine,* April, 1907, p.465.
9. *San Francisco Chronicle,* July 3, 1910.
10. *Nevada State Journal,* June 21, 1910.
11. *New York Herald,* June 25, 1910.
12. *Nevada State Journal,* June 27, 1910.

"Reno, Center of the Universe"

1. *Nevada State Journal,* July 1, 1910.
2. *Reno Evening Gazette,* July 1, 1910.
3. *Hampton's Magazine,* September, 1910, pp.386-396, Lyon, Harris Merton, "In Reno Riotous."
4. *Reno Gazette,* June 24, 1910.
5. *Nevada State Journal,* July 1, 1910.
6. *San Francisco Chronicle,* July 1, 1910.
7. *San Francisco Examiner,* July 4, 1910.
8. *San Francisco Chronicle,* July 3, 1910.
9. *Nevada State Journal,* June 22, 1910.
10. *San Francisco Chronicle,* June 26, 1910.

Moana Springs and Rick's Resort

1. *San Francisco Chronicle,* June 24, 1910.
2. *San Francisco Examiner,* June 24, 1910.
3. *Reno Gazette,* June 25, 1910.
4. *Ibid.,* June 26, 1910.
5. *San Francisco Examiner,* June 24, 1910.
6. *Ibid.,* July 1, 1910.
7. *Ibid.,* July 1, 1910.
8. *Reno Gazette,* June 28, 1910.
9. *Nevada State Journal,* June 28, 1910.
10. *San Francisco Examiner,* June 29, 1910.
11. *San Francisco Chronicle,* June 28, 1910.

12. *Reno Gazette,* June 26, 1910.
13. Cayton, Bill and Robert Obojski, *Boxing Memorabilia.* N.Y. Sterling Publishing Co., 1992. p.43.
14. *Nevada State Journal,* June 25, 1910.
15. *Reno Gazette,* July 2, 1910.
16. Farr, Finis, pp.84-85.
17. *New York Herald,* June 25, 1910.
18. *Nevada State Journal,* July 1, 1910.
19. *Ibid.,* July 1, 1910.
20. DeCoy, Robert H. *Jack Johnson, the Big Black Fire.* Los Angeles: Holloway House, 1991, pp.106-107.
21. Johnson, Jack, pp.172-173.
22. *Nevada State Journal,* July 1, 1910.
23. *Los Angeles Times,* July 5, 1910.
24. Johnson, Jack, p.183

THE FIGHT OF THE CENTURY

1. *Reno Gazette,* July 1, 1910.
2. *New York Herald,* July 2, 1910.
3. *San Francisco Examiner,* July 3, 1910.
4. *New York Herald,* July 2, 1910.
5. *San Francisco Examiner,* July 3, 1910.
6. *San Francisco Chronicle,* July 3, 1910.
7. *San Francisco Examiner,* July 3, 1910.
8. *Ibid.,* July 3, 1910.
9. *Ibid.,* July 3, 1910.
10. *Nevada State Journal,* July 5, 1910.
11. *San Francisco Chronicle,* July 5, 1910.
12. *Reno Gazette,* July 4, 1910.
13. *San Francisco Examiner,* June 25, 1910.
14. *Los Angeles Times,* July 5, 1910.
15. *Ibid.,* July 5, 1910.
16. *San Francisco Examiner,* July 5, 1910.
17. Fullerton, Hugh, p.288.
18. *Ibid.,* p.290.
19. *Los Angeles Times,* July 5, 1910.

20. *San Francisco Examiner*, July 5, 1910.

21. *New York Herald*, July 5, 1910.

22. *Reno Gazette*, July 5, 1910.

23. *Ibid.*, July 5, 1910.

Afterword

1. *New York Herald*, July 6, 1910.

2. *London Morning Post*, July 6, 1910.

3. Fleischer, Nat. *Fifty Years at Ringside*. New York: Greenwood Press, 1969, p.77.

4. Fullerton, Hugh, pp.313-317.

5. *Ibid.*, pp.291-292.

6. *Ibid.*, p.292.

7. *Ibid.*, p.293.

8. *Ibid.*, p.294.

9. Johnson, Jack, p.67.

10. Roberts, Randy, p.151.

11. Farr, Finis, p.134.

12. Roberts, Randy, p.151.

13. Farr, Finis, p.160.

14. *Ibid.*, p.164.

15. Roberts, Randy, p.264.

16. Farr, Finis, p.170.

17. *Ibid.*, p.170.

18. *Ibid.*, pp.170-171.

19. *Chicago Tribune*, May 14, 1913.

20. Farr, Finis, p.170.

21. Roberts, Randy, p.166.

22. *Chicago Examiner*, Jan. 19, 1914; Roberts, Randy, pp.182-183.

23. Johnson, Jack, pp.197-198.

24 *New York Times*, Sept. 15, 1920.

BIBLIOGRAPHY

BOOKS

Ashe, Arthur R., *A Hard Road to Glory. Boxing. The African-American Athelete in Boxing.* New York: Amistad Press, 1993.

Batchelor, Denzil. *Jack Johnson and his Times.* London: Weidenfeld and Nicolson, 1990.

Cayton, Bill and Robert Obojski. *Boxing Memorabilia.* New York: Sterling Publishing Co., 1992.

DeCoy, Robert H. *Jack Johnson, The Big Black Fire.* Los Angeles: Holloway House, 1991.

Farr, Finis. *Black Champion: the Life and Times of Jack Johnson.* New York: Scribner's, 1964.

Fleischer, Nat. *Fifty Years at Ringside.* New York: Greenwood Press, 1969.

Fleischer, Nat. *Jack Dempsey, the Idol of Fistiana.* New York: Bantam Books, 1949.

Fullerton, Hugh. *Two Fisted Jeff.* Chicago: Consolidated Book Company, [1929].

Gilmore, Al-Tony. Bad Nigger! *The National Impact of Jack Johnson.* Port Washington, New York: Kennikat Press, 1975.

Johnson, Jack. *Jack Johnson – In The Ring – and Out.* Chicago: National Sports Publishing Co., 1927.

Lardner, John. *White Hopes and other Tigers.* Philadelphia: Lippincott, [1951].

Lynch, Bohun. *Knuckles and Gloves.* New York: Henry Holt & Company, 1923.

Roberts, Randy. *Papa Jack: Jack Johnson and the Era of White Hopes.* New York: Free Press, 1983.

Samuels, Charles. *The Magnificent Rube; Life and Times of Tex Rickard.* New York: McGraw-Hill, 1957.

Periodicals

Beach, Rex. "The Fight at Tonopah," *Everybody's Magazine*, April, 1907, pp.464-74.

Carr, F. C. "Fighting Father Time," *Colliers*, June 11, 1910.

Davenport, H. "Modern Cave Man," *Colliers*, June 11, 1910.

Farr, Finis. "Jeff, It's Up to You!" *American Heritage Magazine*, Feb. 1964, pp.64-77.

Fyfe, H. Hamilton. "What the Prize-Fight Taught Me," *Outlook*, Aug. 13, 1910, pp.827-30.

Gilmore, Al-Tony. "Towards an Understanding of the Jack Johnson Confessions," *Negro History Bulletin XXV*, (May, 1973), pp.107-108.

Harper's Weekly. "Johnson Wins the Great Fight," July 9, 1910.

Harper's Weekly. "Portrait of Jack Johnson," July 9, 1910.

Harper's Weekly. "Portrait of James Jeffries," July 9, 1910.

Harper's Weekly. "On the Story: the Night the Big Fellow went Out," Dec. 3, 1910, pp.15-16.

Lardner, John. "The Jack Johnson Era of Boxing," *Negro Digest*, Nov. 1949, pp.24-37.

Lardner, John. "The Passing of the White Hopes," *Negro Digest*, Oct. 1949, pp.20-31.

Lyon, Harris Merton. "In Reno Riotous," *Hampton's Magazine*, Sept. 10, 1910, pp.386-96.

Moss, E. B. "In the Ring for a Million," *Harper's Weekly*, May 14, 1910.

Outlook, "Prize-Fight Moving Pictures," July 16, 1910, pp.541-42.

Ruhl, A. "Fight in the Desert," *Colliers*, July 23, 1910.

INDEX

167